# TRIBAL KING AND I

# TRIBAL KING AND I

To You

Dearest Derek,

Hope you enjoy my journey

SHadley (Sue)

**Sue Hadley**

PUBLISHED BY CREATESPACE AND AMAZON.
ISBN-13: 9781984111623
ISBN-10: 1984111620

*Tribal King and I*

I'd like to thank the following people who really made this all happen. This also includes the Minister of education in the Gambia for his kindness. Thanks to Mass Cham the Gambian ornithologist for showing me the way in the Gambia. Thanks also to Dr. Nwaomu, my brothers-in-law; Oney, Sunday, Sylvester; and, my sister-in-law, Ifeyinwa plus all the women of the shrine in Agbor, Asaba, and Illah. Thank you, Colette Bratton my editor, for helping me to make sense of my original diaries and edit this book, plus the Amazon editing team, and of course, big thanks to my father, Shadrach, and my mother, Celia, who always believed in my ability to be someone.

Of course, I need to thank Rob Lycett, my nephew, for designing the covers. And, I cannot forget Bunny for his sheer devotion throughout it all.

# PREFACE

What follows is the pure, innocent, unabridged version of this strange but mostly true-life romantic love story and adventure of just two manic years of my life. One or two names have been changed to avoid embarrassment and to protect those involved in my adventure.

During this story, you grasp not only my outward journey by its miles but also my inward journey to adapt to the culture of the people of Africa. Often, I suffered in poverty amongst them, and I fell in love with a very different man in the Gambia, someone who inherited his title after his father's death.

None of the journey would have transpired if I hadn't gone on holiday to the Gambia with my girlfriends and then moved out there to work temporarily for no pay with an African charity.

This story is a way of remembering and thanking the Nigerian and Gambian people. I hope it raises awareness of endometriosis and its issues, plus highlights the plight of a mixed marriage

It's my first book and I feel that maybe it could inspire others to travel, understand another culture, and to be open to another religion.

Sue Hadley

# CHAPTER 1

# LIFE CHANGES

At last I am going to the Gambia. Now everything is in place. My flight is booked, my large green holdall is packed with a few clothes and some sturdy shoes, the charity work is secured, and taxi to the airport is arranged. All my injections are done, so I am safe to travel. I am now ready to help children in Africa for at least three months. Somehow, I have recognised that this feels like this is my big moment. Maybe it's because I'm now officially middle aged? Perhaps I'm having a mid-life crisis.

I do feel that helping others will help me see my own life more clearly. Perhaps, I will find my own purpose whilst helping others—who knows? My adventure is going to be so different from my normal life, living in a little rented house in Shropshire and working in a stressful job, to moving to a foreign country to do charity work. It involves organising a conference and teaching road safety to Gambian children. My friends think I'm mad, but it just feels like the right thing to do. Who'd have thought that a girly holiday to the Gambia to get over a relationship breakup could lead to this?

The holiday was fabulous, two weeks in Africa. Just resting in the Gambia with my old friends Marian and Helen. It really was just what I needed to get over my recent relationship breakup with Jim. Being cheated upon is bad enough but being cheated on in a small village like Much Wenlock, where everyone knows everyone else's business is even worse—so I needed to get away. He was the reason I had moved from Wolverhampton to Much Wenlock, as it was halfway from his house in Wales. We had admired each other since the age of eleven at school. Then he spoilt it all in more ways than one. Jim was living in Aberystwyth, and I lived in Wolverhampton when we became a couple but commuting every weekend to see each other was a very tiring, so we decided to find somewhere we could live together. We found a beautiful little lodge in Much Wenlock; it was so romantic. We quickly settled into village life and spent many evenings by the log fire in the pub. Unfortunately, Jim had a roving eye, and whilst I was late home from work most weeknights he met someone else. Not just anyone else, but a lady who had stolen a previous boyfriend of mine when I lived in Wolverhampton! With a gut feeling that something was very wrong, I checked my tarot cards one night when Jim was in the pub and was shocked to see what my future held. Firstly, it predicted that I was alone, due to travel, and a great loss and sadness was in the cards for me, with the final card from the Major Arcana being "The World," which represents freedom, travel, and some sort of contribution to society. The predictions came true, when he ran off with her a few weeks later in the caravan we'd purchased together. So really my holiday in Gambia was a godsend, and although I did spend some time writing imaginary letters to my ex-boyfriend Jim, telling him what I really thought of him, most of the time I managed to brush him from my thoughts. The holiday was just the tonic I needed.

Marian, Helen, and I would lie on the beach each day, laughing and joking about our circumstances—good and bad! Then we would do an occasional day trip out to Barra, etc. I told the girls about a letter I'd received from work the day before we flew out to the Gambia, advising me that I was going to have to reapply for my current job as a commercial manager in a college. Apparently, it was a new policy in education. They both agreed that this was a strange thing to have to do to be interviewed for a job you are already doing. Fine, I suppose, if you like your job, but I wasn't too keen on mine. The next day, whilst lying on the beach thinking about my life and about how happy the Gambians seemed with their lives, I said, "You know, I could live here in the Gambia."

"Well, why don't you?" Marian replied, as she lay next to me on the beach.

"The only thing stopping me really is my furniture. Where would I put it all whilst I worked out here?" I said.

"Really?" she questioned. "Your furniture? Well, if that's the only thing stopping you, you'd better start making plans. You can put your furniture in my garage for a while if you need to," Marian said.

"Well, maybe I could do it then," I replied.

I spent the rest of the day pondering, should I really do it? Was now the right time for me to work in the Gambia? Was I too old now that I'd passed the milestone of forty? Could I do some charity work? My mind was whirring, but I felt an excitement about life that I'd not felt for so long! And the more I thought about it, the more I realised that the only thing stopping me doing this was me!

Deep in my heart, I'm an adventurer. A gutsy, backcountry girl from the West Midlands in England, who has always wanted to make good, and who often liked to defy convention.

I hired a bike the next day on that holiday to cycle around the Gambia with a local lad. I hoped to find out more about my potential new home. Unfortunately, whilst on the tour, I hit a sand dune, landed badly, and broke my ankle, and the poor Gambian boy had to run back to the beach to bring the girls to my rescue!

By the time the girls found me, I'd been taken to a private hospital near the beach. As if the situation wasn't bad enough, the girls arrived just as the doctors were doing an operation to turn my foot around (as it was facing the wrong way) and reset my ankle, which was a very unpleasant experience as the doctor hadn't given me enough anaesthetic; so, I passed out with the pain!

I remember the girls saying, "Thank goodness you are insured!"

I spent the rest of the holiday in a hired wheelchair, being pushed around by the girls. We stayed near our accommodation and spent our evenings watching the local amateur music and dancing shows on the holiday park.

We were all sad when the holiday ended, and I really wasn't looking forward to returning home to Shropshire and living alone. All that waited for me was a long, cold winter nursing a broken ankle alone.

CHAPTER 2

# BACK IN ENGLAND

After all that hot weather in Gambia, it seemed really strange to land back in snow at Birmingham Airport—but of course, it was January! I was dreading going back to my empty cottage, so it was almost a relief to be carried off the plane on a stretcher and taken straight to hospital—even if it was for another operation and a new plaster cast.

But a few days later, there I was—back at my own front door of the lodge that Jim and I had rented together just nine months before. He was after all the reason I had moved to Shropshire.

Jim returned two weeks later and stood on my doorstep, asking for forgiveness, assuming I'd let him move straight back in. Well, Jim was in for a shock, because he never got past the kitchen door. I said, "If you have parked your shoes under another woman's bed, you can stay there." He begged and pleaded as he charmed his way into the kitchen and then he tried to make an advance towards me, but as far as I was concerned, I could not trust him. So, I sent him packing back to the other life he had chosen.

As I gazed out of the window at the gardens of that lodge in Much Wenlock, this poem of mine came to mind.

*Snowdrops in Much Wenlock*

*And then the snowdrops came,*
*Bringing you home to me.*
*Lost, sad, spinning nondirectional*

*The snowdrops formed a sheet,*
*As though to make our bed.*
*And oh, that we forbidden*
*Should lie together again.*

*I plucked a snowdrop*
*And thought of our lost love.*
*It seemed so white and bright*
*So full of hope as we were.*

*But snowdrops are a fleeting thing*
*It lived in my vase fresh indoors*
*For just two days, then died.*
*Did your thoughts of renewing,*

*Saving our lost deep love*
*Last so long? I wondered?*

So, I was now living alone, with the plaster of Paris holding my broken ankle together. I couldn't drive, which meant I had to take time off work. I normally liked to be busy, but the forced rest was actually giving me some time to contemplate my life. Although I'd had my run of bad luck, it felt like everything was happening for a reason. If I hadn't broken up with Jim, I might not have gone to the Gambia on a girly holiday. If I hadn't been on holiday, I might not have broken my ankle. If there wasn't going to be a break in my work contract, I might not have thought about taking a career break to go back to Gambia. It seemed like "breaks" were a part of my destiny!

My eureka moment came one day whilst I was upstairs trying to unpack my suitcase, sitting on the floor; then when the pain got really bad, I rested on my bed. I got to the bottom of my suitcase when I found a copy of the *Gambia Daily* the local newspaper in Gambia, owned by the president of the Gambia.

I thought, Well, why don't I go and work in the Gambia when my ankle has healed?

I hopped to the top of the stairs and sat down on my bottom whilst putting my hands out to guide me. I then slid down those stairs. Once at the bottom, I hopped into the kitchen and made a cup of coffee, while my mind raced ahead with all the things I could accomplish out there. I had seen great poverty in this third-world country and knew that the children really suffered out there. Parents had to pay to send their children to school every day, so really, unless those families made money, the children would not even get a basic education. And, all the farming families needed the children to help them to farm, so it was often difficult for many of these children in West Africa to attend school.

As I reread the *Gambia Daily*, there was a picture in it of a teacher at a school in Worcestershire, England, presenting a Manchester United football strip and a football to the children in the Gambia. I found the phone number of the school, rang the headmistress, and told her I'd like to go out and help in any way I could, and she gave me a contact to call at Schools for Progress. This was a Gambian charity that helped educate children through sponsorship from abroad. But the children also needed educating about road safety—as apparently, many children would run after tourist vehicles, risking their lives just to get something, like a pen or some sweets.

I nervously picked up the phone, taking care to support my broken ankle on the chair opposite, and dialled the number. "Hello. Is that "Schools for Progress?"

"Yes, how can I help you, madam?"

"Is that the director of the charity?"

"Yes, it is."

"Well, my name is Sue Hadley. I am a British lady, and I saw a picture in the *Gambia Daily* newspaper of the school in Worcester giving you a football strip, and the teacher gave me your number. I would like to come and work with you there. Would you be interested in that?" I enthused.

The person on the other end of the phone sounded pleased; then he asked lots of questions about my job and qualifications and how I would fund myself. I sold myself on the premise that I would get some funding and products for the charity and organise a conference to educate teachers on facts such as road safety, which would help save more children's lives in the future.

The director offered to call me back when he had thought about our conversation. I'd no idea how long he'd need to think about something like that, so I made myself another drink whilst I contemplated what I'd just done and what I'd possibly just set in motion! I wasn't sure whether to expect a call back the same day or in a few days, but one hour later, I got the call I hoped for. I'm not sure whether it was my business idea and teaching and sales experience that impressed him or just my sheer enthusiasm, but the charity agreed to give me unpaid work in Banjul for three months, right there in the capital of the Gambia, as long as I didn't mind sleeping in their office building as they had no other accommodation to offer.

Also, he only promised a position for three months, which is the usual length of time that volunteers normally worked with them on projects. I would also have to pay my own flights and train the other staff to assist me.

Wow! I was really going there! I quickly rang my family, who, to be honest, weren't as excited or shocked as I would have imagined, and in fact, they were more bothered about how my broken ankle was healing and the fact that I had no groceries for the weekend!

Once I had come off the phone, I started writing to-do lists. There was a lot to do in the next few weeks. In between hospital appointments for my ankle, I needed to inform my employer that I was not going to accept another year there, pack up or sell my belongings, arrange all the necessary flights and paperwork, seek sponsorship, and practise learning to walk again without crutches.

Marian had kept her holiday promise to store my most valuable pieces of furniture and personal effects in her garage whilst I worked away, so all I had left to do now was get the funding for the charity that I'd promised. I needed to plan a mini marketing campaign.

So, I sat and made a list of companies to call. I then wrote a script (of sorts) telling my story and asking for an appointment to meet and present the information. My sales background was coming in very useful! I also contacted a newspaper I'd worked on in the past the Shropshire's daily regional newspaper, the *Shropshire Star*. I remembered they would often report on charity-type stories and even sometimes include a photograph, which would assist to raise awareness and get people to contribute.

Three days later a newspaper photographer arrived, with a journalist, to take details of my adventure. I sat on the wall outside the house for the photo, holding a large atlas and wearing a huge smile. Unfortunately, despite the feature in the paper, no-one rang and offered me any donations, but a local Highways Commission was kind enough to donate some posters, brochures, pens, and paper for me to give out. I was on the right track.

I used my savings to buy a return ticket for £375 and attended an evening course about Muslim culture at Stoke-on-Trent College to gain an understanding of the Muslim religion. I was advised by my college to do this to help me to work with people and not be aware of only the Bible but also of the Koran.

All my friends thought I had gone completely mad and predicted that I would be back home in a week or so, but they still gave me a good send-off in the local wine bar. I must admit that although I was sitting with them in England, my heart was already in Africa.

Marian Myself & Helen in The Gambia

Into Africa

*The plane lifts*
*Flight into Africa*
*At last it's happened*

*Pressures subside, change*
*Homeless, alone, not afraid*
*Excitement, new people*

*The veil lifts now*
*My heart leaps joyfully*
*Unaware, youthful, alive, free*

*Nomadic life such a friend*
*Purposefully now treading*
*My soul renewed African.*

CHAPTER 3

ARRIVAL

After six hours, the plane landed at Banjul airport, and my fellow passengers and I made our way out into the pouring heat. The beautiful bright light of Africa is something to be seen. I could hear drumming, and there were six ladies dancing, dressed in brightly coloured traditional Gambian costumes as I walked past them to find my luggage.

Unlike most airports I'd been to, where luggage arrived on a conveyor belt, this airport had no such technology. Instead, the rest of the passengers and I waited whilst some young men laid our luggage out onto the concrete outside the plane.

Then we had to fumble around, trying to locate all our belongings. I had six boxes of charitable goods that had been kindly donated from Shrewsbury Highway Commission, so it took me a while to locate everything, and in fact, I paid some of the men to help me to get all my luggage together. The charity had promised to send a Jeep to pick me up from the airport, and soon I heard people shouting, "Suzanne, Suzanne, here we are, over here!"

The shouting came from two men, dressed in white T-shirts with a logo and the name "Schools for Progress" clearly emblazoned for all to see. I felt relieved they'd remembered to collect me and excited that my new adventure was all starting to come together.

The men, who introduced themselves as Momodu and Mass Cham, greeted me with smiling faces and loaded all the boxes and my large green holdall onto the Jeep. I sat amazed, as they drove at high speed through the red dusty street of the capital of Banjul.

After an hour, we arrived at an old building in Banjul. The charity's office was on the second floor, and, once we'd got everything up the stairs, I could see that it really consisted of just two manual typewriters, a few old 1950s army-style chests of drawers in dark green, and two old wooden heavy tables with a photocopier with several in trays attached (although there was very little in them).

The electricity seemed to be intermittent, as the old strip lights of the building kept flickering on and off, which was a bit annoying, but I had no choice; I would have to get used to it!

Momodu was a slight man in his early thirties, who was very friendly and trying hard to help me settle in. Mass Cham, well, he was a tall Gambia, bearded man, who seemed to wear a pensive expression. It was difficult to know his age, but I would guess he was around forty-five years of age. He seemed a peaceful, kind soul and had a friendly way about him too. He looked poor, and his clothes seemed well worn, but he had an inner happiness that was so typical of Gambians.

"Come and meet the secretaries," said Momodu.

In walked two young, slim girls in bright-yellow outfits. They bowed and grinned at the floor. As we struggled with the luggage, the two girls ran ahead into the kitchen area and excitedly said, "Look, Suzanne! We have bought baked beans for you, and coffee, and tinned milk. You can sleep in this room and look after the company for us."

I looked at my barren room, which contained a small single bed, a tiny wardrobe, and a wooden desk. There was a small shower room next door. I placed my things on the table and wiped my face with a tissue as the heat and fatigue hit. This was all they could offer, but I was grateful for their kindness.

I wasn't expecting a gift of baked beans, but I was flattered that they had thought of me, especially as the charity had very little spare funds. Gambians are lovely, caring people, so I felt safe with them.

I was escorted into the tourist areas of Banjul to buy food locally, and I spoke to a few other charity workers in the Safari Gardens Hotel; there were lots of high-end hotels, but they all seemed expensive places to drink in and even more expensive to eat in.

Mass was considerate and introduced me to as many people as he knew, but I'm afraid we had to eat beans and rice in the street on the way home.

This was a new experience for me, and it was to be my way of surviving at times there. I was going to have to be careful in the future just where I ate, if I was not to get dysentery. The system was that you queued with the locals and paid around fifty pence (or the equivalent of) for a tasty meal in a paper container. I realised at that moment that money was going to be tight. I would need to budget if I was to stay for my three-month duration or longer.

Mass explained that he lived in a compound, which he described as being like a number of homes built together with shared facilities for all the residents, usually in a walled-off complex, so several people, or families could live together. As his compound was just next door to the charity building, he said if I ever needed anything, to just pop round to him and his father's house next door. That was really comforting to know. As I sensed that the weekends would be quite lonely there.

Mass was quite a local celebrity it seemed, as the local birdman, or as we would say ornithologist, who took people all over Banjul and its villages to see birds and to admire the flora and fauna. He told me he had been listed in all the good guide books on Senegal and Banjul. He spoke good English, so this helped me to understand him, and apparently, his ageing father was the local Iman (holy man) who was greatly respected in the community. It seemed that I'd got very good neighbours.

I was very tired and really needed to rest, so I asked if I could retire early as I needed to unpack and sleep. We walked back through the city streets, and I realised that due to the poor state of the pavements and curbs, it was important to watch where I put my feet if I was not to encounter another broken ankle.

Mass bade me goodnight, and I climbed the stairs to my new office and new home. That is where I met the night watchman. He was the only person on that first-floor office of Schools for Progress there in the middle of Banjul. He was sitting next to his wife and little boy. He greeted me in French, a short slight man—my own night watchman it seemed. I learned that they were from Mali and only spoke in French or Wolof.

Most of the locals spoke Wolof or Mandinka (the local Gambian languages), but it was comforting to know that the watchman was outside speaking French, sitting on the porch with his little kerosene cooker boiling his Gambian tea (called attire), which was cooked in a metal teapot. I fell asleep listening to them whispering quietly as they spent the night on the porch. I lay and thought about this family's life and how they had come to live in such a manner, but I was to learn many things, and I noticed that they seemed happy in their poverty. After such a long, tiring, and exciting day, I was asleep in minutes.

Morning—and the light streamed in through the window of the office, making patterns across the lino-covered floor. I was going to have to learn to love the call of Allah, the melodic call to prayer. Which was always at 5:00 a.m. I managed to get back to sleep, but I was very excited as my adventure had begun. I felt alone but free in that office building. I couldn't wait to check the contents of the charity boxes I'd brought with me, and I started to wonder how I could make a difference in Banjul in this new job.

I looked out of the window at the squalor of Banjul beneath my office building, and I noticed the smells of the local latrines. I realised that I was lucky as I had a flushing toilet, but that was not always the case in Africa as one usually had to have good money to buy one. But as this was a business, it was expected to have a flushing toilet, so I was honoured. Also, to have toilet paper as the locals normally just used a bottle of water and washed themselves with this, using their left hand.

I'd been told that the left hand was considered unclean for this reason. Life was going to be interesting, as I was left handed! I was going to have to learn that, if I shared a meal in a large bowl with Gambians, I was to eat with my right hand only.

Mass & I in Gambia with holiday makers & charity helpers

# CHAPTER 4

# WORKING AND SURVIVING IN THE GAMBIA

The first few months passed quickly. It was already the end of June. I couldn't believe that my three months' stay would soon be up. All the staff had done a lot to help. Plus, I felt I'd learned such a lot whilst working there. I'd soon realised that the two office girls were better at meeting and greeting the teachers at the conference I'd planned, than they were typing up my letters or anything that involved finances. Saying that, I had to admit that I had really enjoyed my stay there.

What I soon learned was that I was still trying to work with an English schedule and expecting any paperwork to be typed by the end of the day. I decided not to let paperwork sit in those in trays until the dust collected on it. The girls worked at an African pace (much slower) it seemed. I was so glad that I had taken my word processor; it really helped—better than the old black classic typewriters that people in The Gambia were making a living off. I seemed to find myself typing late into the night to make sure everything was ready in time.

I often found it so hard to concentrate at times as the charity was so busy with a constant stream of couples filling out forms and being interviewed for the schools in the area, plus the occasional rich tourist or rich businessman who would help to fund the charity or a child. Momodu seemed to be doing most of the face-to-face negotiating and getting people to complete the forms. It was a busy, happy atmosphere mostly. The girls served a lot of the soft drinks, and when these ran out, they would run to the local shop and get malt beer for our guests. I soon learned that this was expected if you were entertaining in Africa. I also had to learn the routine of working with Gambians, who all seemed to get up so early to pray at 5:00 a.m. every day to the call of Allah. It followed that after lunch, the office would be quiet as the girls would eat their rice and snacks, wash their hands, faces, and feet, and pray on their mats. Once this was done, they would often sit at their desks and sleep. They would both drop their heads into their arms on the desk and go to sleep like kindergarten children, snoring across their desks. I was shocked to see this but accepted that this was how it worked in Africa. But even despite the after-lunch naps, I really struggled getting the girls to work at my pace. They would giggle at me multi-tasking and rushing around. They just could not see the urgency of anything. This was frustrating at times, but then I had to remember how lucky I was to be there experiencing all these things. The girls would often say how proud they were to be working with "a two bob" (which is Gambian for a British person)

It seems that the children had learned that if they ran after the trucks and Jeeps, they could beg money off the tourists, who would throw coins and notes out of the windows. Hence the interpretation of "two bobs," known in the past as two shillings hence my new nickname. Thanks to the donations from the Highway Group in Shropshire in the UK, we now had Green-Cross-code-type posters, stickers, and pens, and we were planning to hand these out to the teachers at the conference as this was cheaper and faster than us driving around all the towns to distribute them. They would definitely go in the right hands, and we knew the teachers would love such a treat too. It would really help them to educate the children about road safety, but I was slowly learning more about the business side of things.

I had realised very quickly that there were no spare funds for this conference, so I booked an appointment with the minister of education to try and seek funding for the feeding of the two hundred teachers we had invited and the cost of the hotel. The objective was to get the teachers to cover safety in the home and in the school; also, road safety rules would be taught to get the children to stop them running after trucks down a main road to beg money off those tourists. We had Green-Cross-code-type posters, which were going to be handed out during the conference along with lots of literature. I needed the help of a sponsor. So, I booked an appointment with the minister of education to try and seek funding from him. The conference was coming together nicely. The local police and fire officers had agreed to attend the conference to give speeches about safety for children in the home. Plus, I had arranged for the director of the Gambian TV Station and a representative from UNICEF to come and support us.

That day, I dressed in my pale-green Wallis skirt and white cotton blouse and tied my hair back as the heat was stifling. I realised that it was no use wearing make-up in that heat as it just ran down your face and dripped onto your clothes—very sticky and not at all attractive!

I arrived at the minister of education's office after three unsuccessful trips to try and see him earlier in the month. I thought, Dear God, please let him see me and pay for everything; it will give him loads of prestige and publicity, and of course the whole project will be of benefit to the children. Let's hope that maybe he is a kind Muslim and will help us out because the charity could not afford this event. I also felt guilty that I had more or less imposed the whole mad idea on them all. But my vision of this event happening would not go away. I decided to go and make things happen myself and not sit in the office fretting.

I crossed the busy road armed with a sample of the road safety posters (written in English). I felt that we had a lot of support with our new-found team, just no money to pay for it all. This was my crazy idea and my project, so I needed the Ministry of Education to help out. I had found myself praying more in Africa than ever I had at home for God's help.

As I walked into the minister's office, I noticed that the receptionist was immaculately dressed; she seemed so serene and quietly beautiful, small in stature, petite with her head bowed. After greeting her and announcing that I had an appointment arranged by phone earlier, she bowed her head; then she opened the door. I entered a large office bedecked with gold pictures. There were expensive objects of African art, and they were strategically placed around the shelves. There at the end of the room sat a large dark (almost blue-black) Gambian man in brilliant white cotton silk-and satin robes, with a small white hat perched on his head. This was typical Muslim business man-type of clothing, and it was spotlessly washed, starched, and ironed. He was very tall and large in stature.

He smelt of spicy wooden-smelling aftershave. The smell was vaguely similar to expensive aftershave I'd smelt at airports in the past. His nails were manicured and shiny and buffed to perfection. He spoke with an educated Gambian English accent. Although he could have been a Wolof West African man. This was no quietly meek type of man; he seemed to ooze power and made one feel very small. I felt my knees knocking, but I stood tall and tried not to look him straight in the eye too often as it may appear to be confrontational.

"Greetings, Miss Hadley."

"Greetings to you, sir."

"*Nakasubasee?*" (How are you?)

"*Subasanfee.*" (I am fine.)

"I have heard about your venture at Schools for Progress. People are speaking very well of you "

"Oh, thank you, but I am not a rich woman to be taking care of everything, sir, and I need to tell you all about the project, if you can spare me ten minutes?"

His eyes glanced down at the rolled-up posters.

"Yes, I will, now is that so? Then please state your case, and show me what you have with you," he said.

He leant back in his chair, and I glanced down at his fancy patterned socks and his expensive brown leather shoes. So clean that you could see your face in them. So, I began my speech.

"I have travelled here from Shropshire in England to help the children in the Gambia, and I sought help from the Ministry of Transport manager in England, who has kindly donated posters, pens, books, badges, and papers to give to the children. The reason I am here is that my charity has recognised that the children need to learn about safety in both their homes and in the streets. You see, in England we have the Green Cross code.

"(Pausing for breath.) So, I plan to hold a lecture with key speakers and then give each headmaster who attends the Schools for Progress Conference a box of these free items each. They will then teach the children about road safety and hopefully dispense these to all the children in the schools in their region."

I stopped to get the posters from under my arms and the samples out of my bag. As I held up the poster, he got up out of his chair to read it.

"I do know of this. I schooled in London for a time. The posters are not in our language, but it will help them with their language skills if the teachers teach them to read this in English. Then we could get them translated into Wolof, don't you think?" he commented.

He stroked his forehead to wipe the sweat away and pondered over my strange story during my personal visit to him that day.

"So, you are holding a conference here in Banjul to give this message and these donations. Is that correct?" he said.

"Yes, that is correct. We are expecting over two hundred teachers. It is very exciting. This is a first of this kind. It will be held at the Safari Garden Hotel, or if they cannot accommodate us perhaps another one of the larger hotels here in Banjul. So, what do you think of that?"

"This is a problem." He surprised me by saying.

"What do you mean?"

"Well, many English come here and start something and then go away, and all their good work is forgotten."

I quickly said, "I have thought about this, sir, and I have set up a committee with the chief of Police", chief of Fire, director of Gambia TV, and a member of UNICEF plus a member of Schools for Progress. It is the intention that they can then continue this event every year after my departure. I will give them the telephone number of my contact for the posters and pens in England, so it is possible that this event could continue as a yearly event even if I am not here."

He smiled and said, "This is very good. You must be a big woman indeed."

(This expression means you have money and so are high in status)

I said, "Sir, I may be a tall woman, but I am not big as I need help from you."

"Ha, very funny."

He laughed at my comment about height rather than status. Then his eyes narrowed, and he leant across his desk, intent to hear more.

My monologue began. "Look at this poster. It clearly shows in this cartoon that by educating children, we can save lives. As you know, Minister, in fact good education can save lives. We can only teach this to the children in their schools presently, but they can go home and share this with their families. (I paused). All this means that the children have a chance of being safe and not running after the Jeeps for sweets and getting into accidents. Sir, also that they are not left to sleep with candles burning in their rooms, because if these fall over, perhaps if it's windy, then the candles can prove a fire hazard in the home. Some families in the bush, sir, cannot afford to be linked up to the current electricity supply here, especially out in Barra, for example. These things all need to be discussed at the conference."

I wondered if I had gone too far with this speech, but heck, I needed to knock the socks off him and really touch his heart to help the poor there.

"Sir, I know you are a busy man, but for this to be successful, I need you to do two great things: one, you must come and speak at the conference, and two, I will need to give you the invoice for the conference room and the food, and, sir, I may have to beg for your Ministry of Education department to pay as my charity Schools for Progress cannot afford this."

There was a long silence between us, which felt like the longest silence of my life. I felt the sweat running down my armpits, but it was not sweat from the heat. No, this was the sweat and smell of fear.

He stood up again walked around the poster and said, "I cannot come. I am off to Hajj, Suzanne, the greatest Muslim pilgrimage that every man has to make at least once in his life. But I do think that you are a very brave lady to give me such a big invoice to settle. As I am soon to be on leave, you need to pass that invoice to my office before I travel, and this, by the grace of God, shall be paid. I wish you well."

I did not know whether to bow, courtesy, or kiss that guy. I just could not believe my luck. I said, "You should have a poster for your children perhaps?"

He smiled, showing his large whiter-than-white teeth.

He glanced at his watch as it was near midday, and every Muslim on Friday would close the office to go to the mosque there in Banjul.

I muttered, "I guess it is time for the mosque, sir. I will not keep you. Do I hand the invoice to your secretary later today then?"

"Yes, you must," he replied.

He shook my hand, and I smiled at him in my most business-like manner.

In my delight, I almost flew down those stairs from his office, but I did remember to walk slowly and pretend these things happened to me every day.

The conference was actually going to happen. That was the first time I realised that kindness was there in Africa amongst ministers and business-men and businesswomen.

I really could not believe that he had said yes. I walked across the streets as the loud honking of school buses roared past, full of girls in green-and-white checked cotton dresses and plaits and pigtails. There seemed to be Muslims in white everywhere making their way to the large mosque.

I did not have a cash donation from him, but he was paying for the conference; so, I had no overheads, and I knew the girls and Momodu would be very excited.

Soon, the day of the conference arrived. Over two hundred people came; all the staff except the director of the charity were there. Apparently, he had travelled it was said. The charity workers helped me to settle every-one in, and the girls showed the delegates to their seats. Previously, they had even picked some Gambian glazed cotton cloth for me to have a Muslim-style dress and hat made. I sat on the stage with all the important supporters. Even the head of Gambian TV had now arrived, and the com-pany filmed everyone, including the Police and Fire officers. I was happy that perhaps our sponsor the Education minister's family would see it all on TV whilst he was travelling. I was proud to say that we were going to make that whacky idea that I had in that Shropshire village kitchen really happen.

On the morning of the conference, when all the delegates were arriving, the manager of the hotel had told me not to feed them all until the speeches were completed, as feeding them a heavy meal of fancy rice and chicken would make them sleepy and we couldn't expect them to stay alert and listen through all the speeches after lunch. This was a good piece of advice, so we took it. We then finished all the speeches before feeding them all.

After the meal, the teachers only had to come in to attend the workshop and collect their samples for their schools. They would not be too sleepy for that I hoped. I had to appreciate that many teachers and headmasters had travelled both by bus and boat from Barra to get there, plus they would have a long journey back.

The workshops took place, and the teachers read through the handouts and queued for their boxes. Mid-afternoon, we finally started to hand out the boxes for the teachers to take back to their respective schools.

Yes! we finally had made it all happen. I hoped the children would benefit from this new type of lesson on safety. I heard that the posters and pens were very much appreciated. I did hope that the children would perhaps go home and talk about safety and tell their parents not use candles in their homes whilst they slept. Maybe the children and families would be safer as they slept in their compounds. The other benefit of the conference would be that during the day the children would adhere to the Green Cross Code when they were crossing the road. I thought that maybe even if one child could be saved, we were on the right track. I also hoped that the generations to come would remember the Green Cross Code.

I was so grateful that the minister had assisted by clearing that invoice to make my venue and the hotel food all happen.

As Gambians are a very friendly nation, the farewells were very important, so I seemed to spend a long time shaking hands in that hotel foyer. We began to wish them all much luck with this new venture and give them chance to plan how best to implement our message of safety to all the children across Banjul and Barra.

I stood by the door with Mass and Momodu, and we shook all their hands and bade them farewell. I had learned three Gambian greetings that day:

*Nakasubase*- How is the evening?
*Nanga def*- How are you doing?
*Salaam aleikum* -Peace be upon you

As I would be finishing there at the office in Banjul, I knew that I would need to seek other accommodation. Also, that I would need to find some work if I were to stay on in the Gambia. In Africa, it's often about who you know, not what you know. Mass had already introduced me to the editors of the *Gambia Daily* (an army government paper owned by the president) as I felt I could help there with my experience and knowledge of managing newspapers.

I went to the newspaper office to discuss how I could be of help to them. At my meeting, or should I say informal interview, we had discussed the following areas:

How to increase the number of pages in a newspaper?

How to turn the *Gambia Daily* into a more profitable newspaper?

How I could help them grow the newspaper, increase revenue, and assist with the content—for example, by implementing features into the middle of the paper, which would involve working with the local businesses and getting fresh editorials plus advertisements.

We also discussed my visa stamping arrangements. It was agreed that if I worked with the newspaper, they would pay the cost and arrange that my passport be stamped on a monthly basis. When we were all satisfied with the arrangement, I asked for everything to be put in writing.

Now for accommodation—Mass and I had driven around, asking for a room for me to rent in Bakau town, which he recommended. After several days of help, I found a nice compound near the marketplace and also not far from the bus route into Banjul. I had now paid my first month's rent to

Mama N'jie, who owned a large, friendly compound for locals; so, everything was organised.

It seemed that the newspaper's target market of readers was mainly army personnel, plus a few hundred-general public and that would pay me a small salary and a contract with the Gambia holidaymakers, who read that paper. So, I was set! I now had a job and a decent place to live within commuting distance.

Myself in Bakau

Letter Home:
*Mama N'Jie's Compound,*
*Marketplace,*
*Bakau,*
*Gambia.*

*Dear Mom and Dad,*
    *June 26th 1996.*
    *How are you both there in England? No doubt you are both looking forward to the good weather so that you can work on the allotments!*
    *After much searching, I have found a compound here in Bakau that rents out rooms, and it's clean and fairly cheap. Mom, don't worry because it's not far from Banjul, and I share the area (compound) with several other working women. The room rather resembles a concrete garage.*
    *Mama N'jie, the landlady, has two sons who seem to keep everything shipshape. My bed is a sponge mattress on the floor, and I have a small wooden table (very minimalistic).*
    *I just need to unpack and maybe find a large scarf or two to nail up the windows for privacy, as the window at the back looks on to a dirt track where people pass. Also, the front window looks on to the concrete yard, where all the praying, parties, meetings, dancing, and eating takes place. In fact, all the fun happens here at the very front of my room, so I won't be lonely.*
    *The shower is very basic. It is in the corner of the compound. Also, it seems I share it with all the other lodgers, so I will need to get up early if I am to take a shower and not be waiting around too long before I go off to work in Banjul.*
    *How are all the family, Mom? I do miss some of our English food items like mayonnaise, chips, and coffee, but most of all I miss the intellectual conversations and international media coverage. Mom, I cannot believe I also miss watching TV and visiting the theatres and museums. But you know really, Mom, what I do not miss is the constant stress of England and the sixty-hour week that I was experiencing there at work.*

*Well, I look forward to hearing from you both very soon, and I miss you every day. My latest plan is that I have decided to stay on as long as I can here.*

*Cont'd—Work is going well here. As you know my three months have finished at Schools for Progress, and I have secured some media work (very poor earnings, mind!), but hey, it's here on the Gambia Daily. It's an army newspaper primarily, owned by President Yahya Jammeh. The editor asked me to deliver some training to the new staff. Great news, Mom, as after the training session for all the staff here on layout and legalities, I have also been given permission to interview and employ seven new sales staff to launch a marketing and circulation department to increase revenue and newspaper sales. A very interesting contract. I will not earn an English salary unfortunately; it will be more like a Gambian one, but at least it's a government job, so they will stamp my visa monthly. I can now earn money and support myself here. Progress at last, Mom. Through my contacts with the Gambia Daily, I have also met Babuka Gaye, the director of the radio station; he has offered me some part-time work if I have time there in the afternoons and evenings, selling radio commercials to the local business community. So, I now have two jobs.*

*I will be able to also sell the customers from one media to another, hopefully, if I have enough time!*

*Really, the radio job is a backup; it's commission only, but it's a new venture, and Babuka is so much fun to work for.*

*I'm looking forward to seeing my friend Peter here soon, as he is coming out for a holiday for a couple of weeks; it's his first trip to Africa, so I hope he likes the Gambia. If you see him, Mom, remind him to bring some mosquito spray as this seems to be the land of mosquitoes! Also, toiletries are expensive here, if you can tell him, please.*

*If you have anything you personally wish to send to me, just get Peter to call at your place and collect it, Mom.*

*That is my news for now. Miss, you all.*

*PS: Mom, give my love to all who know me.*

*Love.*

*Sue xxxx*

Mass with birds in Gambia

# CHAPTER 5

# THE GAMBIA

This chapter is for anyone reading who has never visited the Gambia. I feel I need to explain the sights and sounds of the Gambia during the period of the late 1990s. In my opinion West Africa rolled in a rather more exuberant way to the rest of the continent and Banjul was no exception. You could find the echo of a drumbeat around a street corner and the women swathed head to toe in the psychedelic, waxed African printed fabrics that really characterised this most-western edge of Africa. Beggars, and hawkers, offered traditional staples from peanuts to papayas and do still remain there as far as I know. The decorated city streets buzz with music, and everywhere there are boys selling oranges from wheelbarrows, women roasting sweet corn on oil stoves, and outdoor women's hairdressers, who still style your hair and add the most wonderful hair extensions or even shave your head. So, if you are fashion conscious, and you don't mind having your hair plaited in the street, you can arrange that too. The barber shops are also open for business without you needing an appointment, all busy, thriving businesses living off the constant influx of tourists whilst serving the locals. Buses in Gambia aren't too expensive even now, I hear. But they were hot and overcrowded. I often sat next to all sorts of people during the journey. Radio Gambia played in the background, which could be embarrassing especially if one heard one's own advertisement that day that has only the night before been recorded at Radio Gambia offices.

Babuka and I were now working together during the weekday evenings and occasional afternoons at the Capital Radio Station to make the newly sold commercials happen. After we had composed the wording, he would then add the music. I would enter his studio, stand on a chair to reach the microphone, and speak over the music. The reason he said I needed to stand on the chair was because it changed the range and depth of my voice; then magically, hey presto, an advert was born! I then took the advert on a tape to play it to the customer; if the business owner approved of it, I would ask for the money.

Only when Babuka had the money in his hand would he schedule the commercial into his news and music programme. I knew straight away when meeting Babuka in the newspaper offices that I could do some work with him and make a difference. This was partly because Babuka was such a striking and enthusiastic man who had played music for over twenty years. I think I was actually persuaded instantly by his sheer energy about his music and his station there and then to work with him part time.

After an afternoon of walking the streets and sometimes getting exhausted, I would then catch the bus back to Capital Radio, sit with Babuka, and drink cola whilst listening to modern top African tracks and n'daga music.

I needed that cola and to sit in air-conditioned offices, as the work for a British woman who was not accustomed to the heat was exhausting. Obviously, there was no car involved in the job, so I needed to walk many miles and knock on a lot of doors before anyone bought those radio advertisements.

Meanwhile back at the Schools for Progress charity, Momodu was now liaising with two German ladies who had flown in as they owned the charity; apparently, they were informing him on how to administer the paperwork for the children to be sponsored. We had done a lot to get a system in place during my three-month placement there at the charity. I hoped that we had helped to raise awareness, but the charity really could not afford to give me accommodation there now as my office room was needed to put files in. They were sorting out the Director's office also, now that he had travelled. The idea of the big sort-out was so that the girls could so some filing and create a contact list of potential sponsors. I really preferred to be working for myself where I could make a difference on the radio there.

The boat to Barra (Gambia)

# CHAPTER 6

# PETER'S ARRIVAL

"Greeting, Mama N'jie."

"Nakam," she replied as I passed her in the yard.

"How are you?

"Fine, how are you?"

"Well, fine too, but just to tell you that Peter, my friend, arrives from the UK this week," I said.

I then handed over thirty-five pounds for his accommodation (which Mama and I had agreed on earlier that week). She counted the notes and stuffed them into her wrapper (skirt) under the waistband, as she made her way across the yard to her house.

It was July 1996, and Peter was to sleep in a small hut in the courtyard of Mama N'jie's compound in Bakau. As it was a white man she did not know entering the compound, Mama N'jie eyed me suspiciously, but I said, "He is just a friend who is here as a tourist, and he is only here for two weeks."

She didn't look convinced but pushed the money into her pocket and thanked me anyway. The huts reminded me of the concrete garages you see on housing estates, except these each had one window. Inside Peter's hut there was just a sponge mattress on the floor and a small table. He'd have to share the communal shower facility with me and the six other women tenants. Most of my neighbours were street traders who visited Ghana to gather rolls of cloth to sell in the marketplace, so they led busy lives and weren't that interested in my comings and goings. Some of the women were collected in black taxis by rich men and then delivered back in time for the call of Allah at 5:00 a.m. I think they did business with the rich tourists in the hotels.

One or two of the ladies had small children but not a husband in sight. In fact, the only two men in the compound were Mama's two tall teenage sons, who dealt with any intruders or people who didn't pay their rent. It felt like a safe place to live. We had a very large cast iron gate across the compound to stop unwanted guests appearing. We really led a sort of happy life here even though all of us struggled for money. The good thing about the compound was that it was only twenty minutes into Banjul, the capital, by bus.

I was hoping that Peter would not be too disappointed with these very basic almost-primitive surroundings as this is was his first real experience of a third-world country. Maybe he was used to much finer things in life than a sponge mattress on the floor. In order to try and make things homelier for him, I covered the mattress with a couple of pieces of Gambian cloth, which the women had sold me. I thought how it was going to be strange for Peter. A single man in a foreign country that was completely alien to him. He would be surrounded by six women, strangers in the compound. What would they think of him? And how would Peter react to them? Especially if they showed any physical interest in him.

It certainly would be a different life for him—spending the next two weeks under a mosquito net, with no running water and only rice, fish, and vegetables to eat most of the time. I knew he was soon to recognise what it was like to live in a third-world country. I knew he would be shocked by the heat, dust, and poverty that we didn't experience in England. Thinking about Peter's reactions made me realise how I'd adapted to life in Gambia, and things that seemed strange when I arrived three months previously, I now just classed them as normal and didn't give them a second thought.

Let me describe my dear friend Peter. He was a tall, friendly, brown haired, extrovert, around twenty-eight years of age. Born in Warrington to a middle-class family, he was curious to see me and my new life in the Gambia. I was also keen to know what he thought of it all. Whether he would notice how I had adapted to my environment. How I had found work and my new thoughts on life. He would be shocked to see my appearance with my long, brown hair extensions—which of course were false. It had been newly purchased in a packet from the market for the equivalent of ten pounds. It was a very different look to my English style where most of the time my hair was tied back and business like. But because of the heat there, it was the only way to keep my own hair looking decent. I had also lost weight and looked very different from the friend he had known.

I'd arranged for my new friend and colleague from the charity, Mass, to help me collect Peter from the airport. It was very kind of him to help, as he was usually very busy not only helping the charity but accommodating the many birdwatching tourists who flew in weekly from all over the world. Often, we would see them arriving with their ornithological equipment but needing the tour guides to help them navigate around the mangrove swamps. They would be taking photos and recording Gambia's five hundred and sixty bird species, so I knew a bird trip for Peter with Mass would be planned.

Mass arrived in a borrowed open-top Jeep, which had seen better days, but it would get us to the airport. He had a spare can of petrol in the back of Jeep in case of emergency. I always felt safe travelling with Mass as he spoke Wolof, the local language, which made travelling through Gambia so much easier.

When we arrived at the airport, we could see Peter looking completely stressed, as he tried to explain to the two immigration officers his reasons for visiting. Unfortunately, filling out the form for entry into Gambia was proving an issue, as they were asking him what hotel he was staying in. But as I hadn't sent him the full accommodation details, he was having a problem! Fortunately, Mass charged in and explained everything whilst Peter and I tried to find his luggage amongst the massive pile of cases on the floor.

The whole airport was small, run down, and not very modern at that time. Peter hugged me but kept one eye on the pile of cases. The beads of sweat trickled down his face—it was over thirty-two degrees that day, but he seemed to be taking it all in his stride. We all jumped into the Jeep and chatted whilst negotiating the traffic through the heat and dust.

Suddenly, the car stopped. "Why has he stopped?" enquired Peter.

"I think we have run out of petrol," I replied.

"Suzanne, I go now to put fuel in Jeep, OK?" said Mass.

He quickly unloaded the petrol can and filled up the tank from a very larger container at the back of the Jeep whilst Peter looked on in astonishment. Feeling embarrassed at my poverty, I managed to make a joke of the incident. Fuel, coffee, medical bills, and travel expenses ate hard into my savings and my African salary. I had to learn to live on what I had in cash daily. This consisted of living on around one English pound a day. My mother would send me a little amount per month that I had in savings.

When we finally arrived in Bakau at my compound, Peter threw his case on the sponge mattress and immediately asked me to take him to the Gambian shower in the yard. Mass lit a cigarette and sat on a small stool in the yard and looked on kindly. He was waiting for the scream as the very cold water hit Peter. The African-style shower has a simple bucket placed on a lever, which one pulls to empty the bucket. This then forces the bucket's contents out over your body. This is a sight to behold.

"Aaargh! It's bloody cold," said Peter. Mass and I laughed out loud. This was the locals' response to new people arriving in that compound. Peter was going to have to adapt very quickly if he was to fit in.

Later that evening, I took Peter out for a drink so that he could buy a meal at one of the hotels, and he finally seemed happy and relaxed. I think he had taken to the Gambian way of life very well for his first day.

The next morning I'd arranged for Mass to call for Peter in the compound to take him out for the day birdwatching whilst I worked.

I was sure Peter would have a great day. Mass was a perfect host, and he'd planned a busy day. However, I got a shock when I returned home at 3:00 p.m. to find Omar, a tall dark, intelligent Gambia man in his twenties, now one of my salesmen from the newspaper, running into the compound as I returned. "Suzanne, we need to go to the jail very soon, big problems," he said.

"What do you mean? What's happened?" I replied.

"Mass has been arrested for not paying his parking ticket by the police, and he is in a cell. Peter is waiting to tell you," blurted out Omar.

Just then Peter came out, looking very shocked and quite pale.

"Sue, they just took Mass away and left me there in Serekunda alone… and err, I have walked over three miles to get back here. It was really scary as the police were wearing guns! I think if you call the police or visit, we might get some idea what is happening, don't you think?"

"So, OK. Don't panic, Peter. It's just a fine, something simple. After all we know that he is not a criminal." I heard myself say in an attempt to calm Peter down.

"Oh crikey, but I didn't have enough Gambian money on me to help him to pay up and get out," Peter explained.

Poor Peter—he must have been terrified. This wasn't the kind of Gambian experience I wanted him to have and felt terrible about what he'd been through. I sat on the chair and began quickly thinking what I could do to help Mass. I had the solution right there under my bed—some Gambian money.

"Don't worry, Peter I have some spare cash. This is no big thing." I then quickly ran to my room, closed the door, and extracted some dalasi's. I strolled over to Omar, who was smoking a cigarette, leaning against the compound wall, and handed him the bundle of notes, trying to keep my calm and look unafraid of what may happen if we left Mass languishing in the jail with armed policemen.

"So, Omar, my dear friend, can you please go to the jail with this money and pay what they need? Don't tell them a British lady paid, or they will charge you more, I am sure. Oh, and, Omar, also pay your bus fare and bring him back please."

Omar nodded, eager to help out.

"Thanks, Omar, and oh, please do take fifty dalasi for your trouble, thank you very much," I said.

Omar Dem ran straight out of Mama N'jie's compound, leaving a trail of red dust behind him. I trusted Omar and knew he would chat to the police officers and give the correct amount of cash to pay off Mass's fine.

Peter looked shocked. "Just like that, they will let him out? Do you think that will work? You know, Sue, they seemed strict with guns and everything. It was really scary stuff."

"Yes, it will be fine. Listen, Peter, just settle down, and everything will be all right. This is Gambia and it will all be over soon all be over soon. It's safe here, really it is!"

I passed him his cigarettes, and he lit one for the both of us as our hands were shaking. I was really an occasional smoker then, but I began to realise as he walked away in his khaki shorts and his newly burnt pale arms, smoking his cigarette, that I had changed. An event like this in the past would have been a big thing, but now, after even a short while in West Africa, I was learning to manage things better.

Yes, a real shift had occurred. I felt more African than English, and I was even beginning to think like an African. My beliefs were changing. My health was an issue, though, as I hated taking those awful malaria tablets as they were giving me nightmares, but according to the doctor, they were important if I was to keep the malaria at bay. I was to learn the hard way about that bad idea of mine to not take those tablets anymore.

But I had found that you soon learn that money is the only thing that talks in this kind of situation in Africa, and if someone paid Mass's fine, he would be released.

Maybe Mass would be a little shaken, but he would be fine. Tomorrow, it would be all over. At least Peter would be able to say he had a real African adventure.

Mass arrived back later that evening with Omar at the compound, and they sat outside in the yard on the wooden stools outside Peter's room, going over the situation. Then, as the light began to fade, they spoke in whispers, as many of the women in the compound were putting their children to bed. We swotted the mosquitoes that buzzed around us.

I reminded Peter to change into clothing that covered his legs at night. Many Gambians seemed to smoke, and when I once asked why this was so, they replied it was to keep the mosquitoes at bay. There was something quite different about purchasing cigarettes there in the villages, because you could buy just one cigarette if you were hungry and broke from the local shop. This would have been unheard of in the UK.

Later Omar and Mass bade us goodbye and made their way back to Banjul. Of course, Peter talked about that a lot during his stay as it was a rude awakening for his second day, but as the holiday continued, he settled down, and Mass and he went on more than one trip out to see Latrikunda, Serekunda, plus remote villages and tourist birdwatching spots like Lamin Lodge.

I didn't expect Mass to pay me back as he was very broke, so I never mentioned it again. Soon, Peter was heading back to the airport, bidding me farewell whilst hugging me and thanking me for a real adventure and wishing me well. After I left Peter at the airport, I caught the bus back home to my compound as Mass couldn't get the Jeep that day as the charity had already booked it out for school visits. I felt sad on that bus. I was going to miss really talking to another English person. My local friends could speak English quite well, but there's more than sharing a language in talking I found. It was about having a shared past and a shared culture. I realised, having Peter stay, how much I missed being able to use English sayings and certain humour and jokes that are very specific to us Brits. But, no time for sadness and regrets. I needed to concentrate on earning money. Paying Mass's fine had eaten into my already-low cash emergency fund, but I knew in my heart Mass would not be able to ever pay me back. So, we all just moved on and put it down to bad luck.

Even though I was working hard there, at least I'd have the weekends to recover and rest. Peter's stay had made me realise how "Gambian" I'd become in my attitude to events, money, etc. So, I cheered myself up thinking about how happy I was, or was I? I still felt lonely and longed to meet someone very special. I was hoping that would happen soon.

Peter Lyons in Gambia

*Expat*
*Here you are on foreign ground*
*Africa in all her beauty is here*
*Let her craziness unfold*
*Be happy and content to have arrived*

*Hoping for finer things*
*Wealth and riches no longer important*
*Just forget the Western ways*
*Be happy and content to make a difference*

*Don't grumble and moan with the expats here*
*For what should or could happen*
*You are here to give of yourself with passion*
*Be happy and content to teach and inspire*

*Ever joyful as you mingle amongst these tribes*
*Time is a gift use it well here*
*Write of all the people and their ways*
*Be happy to learn about strange cultures*

*Do not long for English comforts*
*Remember why you came here*
*Follow your path wherever it may lead*
*Be happy to contribute*

*Live for now, not for an English life*
*Forget your old; love life and its perplexity*
*Leave it all behind in its dryness*
*Be content to be open and aware.*

*Let the small voice within comfort you*
*Reflect on the wonders of this new climate*
*Meet new people along your path*
*Be content to be African now.*

View from the office back window in the Gambia

# CHAPTER 7

# THE MEETING

It was Friday afternoon in late November, and the sun was scorching everyone in sight there in the Gambia. But it doesn't matter where you are in the world; that "Friday feeling" is the same. The delightful thought that work is finished for a few days.

I had just finished my work in Banjul and had made my way home to Bakau, where I had decided to go to the beach to get my white body a little browner and get some solace from the madness of deadlines on the newspaper and the radio station.

I carefully picked my way along the clifftops, wearing a T-shirt and shorts, with my favourite desert boots and my thick woolly grey socks. I felt like a fell walker, traversing my way along the sheer clifftops until I arrived at a lonely area of the beach along the Bakau shoreline. Despite being well into the Gambian tourist season, there wasn't another tourist in sight. Glancing around at the magnificently tall palm trees there, I suddenly felt calm and rested in Africa's beauty. I was at one with nature.

Many of my friends and relatives in England would give anything to escape the rat race, but I was able to because I was now completely free— no children to restrict me and no husband or boyfriend to answer to. I glanced along the beach and saw only one other white person in the distance, a man reading a paperback book, keeping himself to himself.

I remember looking away from him at that point and thinking about his innocent comment. Then something strange happened kinaesthetically; the hairs on my arms lifted, and a cold breeze seemed to run over me. This was one of my own signs that this was a psychic encounter. I knew at that very moment in time that this man was a very psychic person. Maybe, I had met my life partner. I was trying to hold on to reality and not get carried away with this psychic message. I could feel myself being swept away by this wild Aborigine-looking man. Me, a sensible middle-class woman, even a career lady in England. My heart was beginning to rule my head. There was no escaping it. I could hear myself asking inane questions like "When is your birthday?" and Bunny replying, "Oh, June 14th." Then I began thinking, He's a fellow mercurial star sign. My mind raced over the characteristics: air sign, a communicator, best suited to a career as a journalist, teacher, writer, and a creative sign, blah, blah. My thoughts were seized with positives of how he could be just right for me! What an interesting quiet manner he had. He seemed to be an introvert.

We talked nonstop until the sun began to set around us. The man reading the paperback book along the beach had long since departed. We began to discuss art and music and poetry, and his mind was razor sharp. I had seen an interesting piece of driftwood on the platform where we sat; it lay with some old coconut husks in an interesting and artistic form, and it had caught my eye earlier. I stood up to show him for a second opinion. As he stood next to me, I must admit I found myself checking his height, subconsciously sizing him up, some women might say. Whilst I'm five feet eight inches tall, he was six feet tall, with a taught torso and slimmer than me and with gorgeous white teeth, the kind with a natural gap in them, which is an African sign of beauty.

As we approached the steps, Bunny held my hand; contact was established. Suddenly our physical barrier was removed. I felt light headed and excited, realising that I was beginning a relationship, yet I knew instinctively this was no ordinary relationship. I could feel my body tingling with excitement. He never stopped smiling, and I noticed when he laughed, he had the kind of laugh that sounded as though it didn't belong to him. The hours passed away so quickly. We watched the sun setting over the sea, creating a labyrinth of intricate shades of yellow and gold around us. We gazed at it together, still not daring to touch one another, yet longing to. Bunny offered to show me the old hotel where he and his band Sky

Juice lived. I got dressed, packed my beach bag, and accompanied Bunny towards the concrete steps that led to the Tropical Gardens Hotel.

That weekend, we never left each other's side and were together from morning until night. I joked to Bunny about being kidnapped. No-one knew where I was, and I didn't care. I was falling in love and having fun. Bunny played his guitar and sang to me as we sat cross-legged in his room, comfortable with each other, rapport established. It was as if I knew that instantaneously we had fallen in love. It seemed we were mentally and physically ensconced.

Monday morning soon arrived, and I rushed home to shower and change. Bunny was rushing to shower too, in the much-abandoned building of his hotel. He was eager to write more music and compose more songs—all about love this time.

We dated for several weeks before I was ready to invite Bunny to move into my compound as my partner. Local Gambian custom needed to be adhered to, so it was important that Mama N'jie accepted him. They had suffered some bad experiences in the past. She informed me that in the room next to mine some Nigerian tenants had sold a fake diamond to a local jeweller. The local business owner had paid thousands of dalasi's for it before he discovered it was fake. The two Nigerians escaped during the night to the airport, it was said. Even with all the money they had made, they still disappeared owing rent to her for their lodgings. The jeweller discovered that he had been duped and that the diamond was fake and came back shouting and asking everyone where the Nigerians were, but to no avail.

I had to explain to her that Bunny, although Nigerian, was not like that, and we would not owe her any money or invite anyone to our room without consulting her. I felt as though I had inherited a new strict mother there in the Gambia.

After I introduced Bunny to her, thankfully she allowed him to move in. The next evening, she had some fish and rice flavoured with Maggi stock cubes, which we ate from a large tin bowl communally by hand. It was lovely to see all the women in the compound sitting with us by candlelight and sharing the food. A real celebration of my new love. Bunny said he felt accepted, but he explained to me when we went back to our room that this was not always the case in Gambia.

When he arrived, he had been warned that Nigerians and Gambians often did not mix very well as Gambian men felt that the Nigerian boys stole the female tourists from them. I chose not to get involved with the African prejudices.

Bunny and I on the beach

*Oblivious*
*He watched her sleeping*
*The sea thundered into the shore*
*She was oblivious to it all*
*Their eyes met as he approached*
*Into her world he stepped*
*Like a spider into her web*
*Loves newness and happiness*
*Ensconced by it all*
*Love took its shape*
*In the heart of Africa*
*Sun setting around them*
*Its orange and red shadows observed*
*They climbed the steps together*
*Hand in hand, joined as one*
*Love's link established*
*Oblivious.*

CHAPTER 8

# THOUGHTS

I'm not sure what hour they began, but I remember the date clearly—
Tuesday, December 10th 1996. I'm talking about the doubts. It's as
though a small comment from Billy, an expatriate boy who had called into
my office at the *Gambia Daily* to look for work, his comment somehow
tarnished my thoughts. Like a kiddie who has heard a rumour that Father
Christmas isn't real I was in total disbelief. I felt that Bunny's relationship
with me had a childlike innocence until that point. Then I felt that fade
away, and a doubt about Bunny and our pure, clean, innocent love came
upon me.

Billy and his off the cuff sarcasm warning me to be careful as he suggested that all Africans want something from you if you are foreign, such as
your money invested in them or their country. You see Billy truly believed
that these people, as he called them, were like that. Perhaps all Africans
ever want from any of us is our money?

Billy passed me on the fire-escape staircase that stood outside our
office in Banjul, with a kind of look of disdain. It was very unnerving. Had
I made a mistake? Was he right? He really had planted that seed of doubt. I
was using all my savings up supporting Bunny at that time, but I felt Bunny
would soon give it back when he found more work.

After much thought, I decided that Billy was just being prejudiced and
maybe he was jealous. Also, they had employed him to work there, and as
such I decided that I would not tell him my business from now on. I also
did not want to listen to his opinions. Or his stories of how many African

women he had slept with and paid money to. He reckoned they were all after his wallet.

I hated to think that there was any chance that this love between Bunny and I was all in my head and that Bunny was scheming or wicked in any way.

I couldn't wait to see Bunny after work that day, and I rushed to meet him in the ruins of Tropical Gardens Hotel. He looked troubled when I arrived. He hugged me and asked if I was well. I nodded yes, as I'd decided not to tell Bunny yet about Billy's comment. He said he felt like I was sand slipping through his fingers and that soon I would leave and go back to England, back to the old life I'd known before, back to British normality. Bunny told me that he felt frustrated about us, as he wanted us to be together forever.

Gosh, Bunny was moving in fast on me. We started to chat about our potential new life together, about maybe getting married and living in Nigeria; some really big plans were being aired in the sea breeze that day.

My concern was about money. How would we manage in Nigeria? I loved him dearly, but Bunny and I were often like children when we were together, a bit reckless in our thinking about how we'd run our lives. Practical words like "career," "work," "visas," "permits," "marriage licenses," and "birth certificates" were discussed whilst we ate our French stick of bread with a juicy red melon. I felt it was right to marry Bunny and even try for a child, but I worried about the fear of the unknown. What if I didn't like it there in Nigeria? How would I leave the country if I had no money left?

How would it look if I went home and said it hadn't worked out? How could I handle the shame? What if I couldn't conceive? I would be phoning my mother about our life when I went to the office the very next day. I had to make up my mind and stick with that decision now, not tomorrow. But why was I so confused?

That night I was lying next to Bunny in my compound. He was fast asleep, but I felt the presence of something inhuman, like an evil spirit, something really sinister entered the room. I couldn't see it, but I could feel it. I have always been sensitive to presences—good or bad—but this was altogether something else. It moved around the room with its tremendous strength; it moved past me, and I knew it was after Bunny, who was sleeping on the other side of the bed. I felt that I was somehow there to protect Bunny from this. It couldn't seem to get past me. It was after him. I knew it. It seemed to have no human form, and a fear gripped me. I lay still and waited for what seemed forever. Then, I felt it had left the room.

But suddenly I could smell smoke; in fact, I couldn't breathe for it. I shook Bunny and said, "Bunny, Bunny, wake up."

"What's wrong?", he shouted.

"Something is on fire; it smells as though someone has lit a fire right outside our room."

Bunny jumped out of the bed and looked through our window at the iron door leading out onto the courtyard of Mama N'jie's compound.

"I can't see anything. I'll check the other window," he said.

Dawn was just breaking as Bunny walked across the room. Then suddenly he yelled, "It's our room! The smoke is in our room."

I jumped up and ran to the end of the bed, where I could see thick smoke emerging. There was our orange bath towel going up in smoke. It had fallen on the mosquito coil which was burning on the floor at the bottom of the bed. (mosquito coils are similar to joss sticks and remain alight all night) A large black mass of burned towel was causing thick smoke to emerge and almost suffocate us. Bunny grabbed what was left of the towel and threw it out of the door. As the light streamed into the room from the door being left ajar, I noticed something very strange. The wind had blown a pack of playing cards across the yard of the compound, and the Four of Clubs lay on our step. I normally read tarot cards, not playing cards, but the meanings can be interpreted just the same. It said, "Power house," you have a lot of work to do. "The workings of some sort of power are around you." In other words, there's lots of business to do.

So, there was the meaning for the fire; it was to give us a message to go outside to read the cards. Psychic messages come in many forms. This was just one of the many ways we would receive information to guide us on our path to help people. My role was to be the one educating people, and his role was to lead his people but neither of us knew how or where.

I had already begun a diary at that point as the psychic happenings were coming so fast since I had met Bunny. It was as though he helped to attract these messages. Sometimes when I walked down the red dusty streets of the Gambia with him, I felt I was walking with an old soul and that we had known each other before and this was a repeat of an old life. I know this is difficult for people to understand, but the feelings were so acute that I could not deny them. My dreams were becoming very vivid, and not all were good, but nevertheless they were prophetic at times.

This was not really that new to me, as since the age of three I had always had visions and messages. It ran in both sides of my family—we called it the "gift," and my mother had never made fun of my messages as she herself seemed too often to "just know" things. Throughout my life, I had many experiences of feelings and had experienced life on different levels, creating a much-wider knowledge of people and life for me. Unfortunately, most of the time I did not disclose these messages or gut instincts for fear of what people would think. We all have a sense of intuition, a kind of sixth sense, but not everyone uses it. However, by the time I reached twenty-three years of age, I couldn't hold it down anymore, and my intuition told me to go to a shop and seek, seek! What sort of message was that? But still, I walked into W. H. Smiths in Wolverhampton. I soon found myself in the occult divination and spiritual section, looking at the bookshelf. I had been brought up as a Christian. This was crazy. There, I saw a pack of "Rider Waite" tarot cards that were written in French. I would need to study these very hard and translate the meanings, but I knew I needed to buy them. I had no idea how to use those cards, but over the next two years, I taught myself all about them and all their meanings. I was fascinated and a little confused because dabbling in the occult went against my Christian beliefs, but still the messages would come, telling me about births or deaths and other good and bad things. Yet sometimes I'd have nothing happen for three or more years—it was very strange indeed. As though the gift lay dormant.

Two years later whilst driving, I passed a clairvoyant's office in Wolverhampton and had the urge to telephone the number that was displayed above the shop. I learned that he offered psychic parties, where he'd come to your house and give messages to you and your friends. So, I booked him there and then and arranged for some friends to come around one evening, as more than anything I felt I needed to speak with someone on this subject.

When he arrived, he turned out to be quite a theatrical character, with dark hair and a rotund belly. He spoke in a rather loud grand voice, and, to be honest, he was a little bit scary. My friends sat in the kitchen drinking wine and giggling whilst I ushered him through to the lounge to chat with him. The first thing he said to me was "You are one of us, an old soul. It's a valuable gift, but you must use it carefully. It is sometimes good, and sometimes it is not. But I feel you know all these things, but you need to hear them from others in your field."

I felt the hairs lift up along both arms and at the back of my head. I was energised. After he'd done all our readings, and he stepped out into the dark night, I knew I would see this man again. In fact, I saw him at several psychic events, and he always nodded to me as he passed.

I would often try and block the instinct as I was working full time, and I did not want to get too wrapped up in psychic messages. I always had this feeling that one day I would wake up, and it would be gone like a magical thing. I also felt guilty about my own Christian beliefs. So, I started to go to church and pray again, and all the gifts seemed to rest for a while. My mind moved back to Bakau, and Bunny murmured in his sleep right next to me.

As I lay next to him, I stroked his naked back, marvelling at the smoothness of his skin. He wriggled closer to me as our bodies spooned together. I just gazed at him as the light streamed into our room, wondering if his life had similar coincidences and whether he had gifts that had ever troubled him. I lay there pondering on this but eventually told myself, "Time to think of the future not the past," as I concentrated hard on falling back to asleep.

# CHAPTER 9

# PROPOSAL

The intensity of our relationship was increasing. Even when I left his side to go to work, I felt a wrench. I was now charged with a new energy. This new love had given my confidence a real boost, and I'd somehow gained youthfulness and a sense of purpose. Today was a nice, hot, sunny day, so I had my beach bag sitting alongside my business folders so that I could rush to the beach to see Bunny after work. I arrived there at 5:30 p.m. Bunny was sitting looking out to the sea. I called him from the cliff-tops, and we ran to greet each other. We walked along the shoreline, barefoot, our long hair blowing behind us in the sea breeze, completely alone on our beach. That's when he said it. Such an unexpected request, spoken with love and sincerity.

"Sue, will you marry me and bear my children?"

"Oh, Bun, it's all so sudden. Give me time to think."

He kissed me passionately and agreed to ask me the next day when I had considered his request.

That night I couldn't sleep, thinking about this offer of betrothal. He is a lot younger than me, I thought. How will I produce his child? I was fighting against being sensible and the sheer passion of this love.

The next day when I arrived at the beach to meet him after doing my shopping in a haze, I could see him facing the sea as the tide was quickly coming in. I called his name, and he turned to run towards me.

The waves crashed into the shore. It was nearly deafening but so romantic. I'd met my black prince. I had made a commitment to an African man, a Rastafarian. Bunny had mentioned his religion was that of an African

Traditionalist, but I did not fully understand it all. He said they believed in spells, rituals, and sacrifices to honour their gods. Divination was by the Ifa method, I learned. It was all going to be very different indeed for me. Deep inside something told me that it was right and spiritually meant to be. Even if it meant that I was going to witness a strange and different religion. Bunny and I began to discuss this area of our belief system. Bunny explained that he originated from a town called Illah in Delta State, Nigeria.

He was the head of a large family of ten children, and his father was the "King of Illah," as well as being a great chief priest who had fifteen fellow chiefs serving under him. Bunny, it seemed, was the next in line to the chief and king title. I could not believe what I was hearing. I felt overwhelmed and confused! How could I be of assistance in such a lifestyle when I did not even speak "Igbo," his native language? Bunny said that after three long years of searching, he had found his jewel. He said he did not want to tell me all about himself when we first met in case I ran away. I had fallen in love with a man who I thought was an out-of-work musician, not a prince. I kept thinking that perhaps many women back in his hometown might want to marry him to be with him just for his status. He knew that I had known nothing of this when we met, which signified he felt that our love was honest and true. His sole purpose of travelling to the Gambia was that he wanted to become a reggae star before he took up his crown and chieftaincy title. As I suspected when first speaking to Bunny, this was no ordinary man. I began to feel anxious about all the responsibility and strangeness of this new way of life being offered to me. I said, "Bunny, can you please ask me again tomorrow, as I need to think about all this?" He looked puzzled but agreed to do just that.

I had joked with my friends about finding a black prince and disappearing across the Sahara, now look at me, being asked for my hand in marriage by a real prince!

Was I doing a Shirley Valentine? Was I having a midlife crisis? Had I lost my senses? I was over forty, single, a British lady in the Gambia. But I decided that I didn't care, as it all felt completely right. But I did need to sleep on this new information about kingdoms—gosh, what a lot to take on!

The next morning, I awoke and I rushed off to work early on the newspaper before Bunny woke, not wanting to discuss again our very deep conversation that had taken place on the beach. I now needed solace to think on that bus journey to work and to decide what I wanted and what I needed in this affair and, heck, to give Bunny all the answers he sought. I was still trying to understand Bunny's world.

Work passed in a haze that day, as I had so many things running through my mind. It seemed advertisement deadlines were the least of my worries. Later that day I handed in a tape to Babuka on my second job at the radio station with a note to Babuka, explaining that the bank (my new customer) had agreed on the new advertisement and would he please excuse me that afternoon from recording the advert with him as I had a very important date!

I was keen to get to that beach again to be with Bunny once more and hear more about Bunny's life back home and what he would expect my role to be.

We met on the beach and walked together—him with his guitar under his arm, occasionally sitting on the beach to serenade me with his love songs. I asked him more about his life in Nigeria. I had to know what I was letting myself in for. I listened intently as Bunny spoke.

"Well, it is not like it is, in the UK Sue, or here in the Gambia, with many tourists. In Nigeria we have tourists there, and sometimes it's a dangerous place. We have a large population of over a hundred million people. My life is very different as my father is very important in our tribal religion, and he has seven shrines and many houses. My life is never really my own as I am required to be on duty and serve my people. That's why this time here in the Gambia is such an important and glorious time for us, because we have time to be alone."

Bunny was full of these large, convincing monologues. When I asked him why he hadn't married a girl from home, he said, "I wanted to find my own bride who would love me for myself—which is what has happened with us here."

My main worry was what I'd do for a living while he was serving his people, and Bunny advised that I should just be near him, listening and learning about it all. He said, "Well, you have to be at my side to hear my problems and share my joys, as you will be my wife."

He explained, "I will not be able to be a musician there as I am not expected to work. You will assist me to run my kingdom and encourage people to join our shrines. You are a marketing person, and I need you to do this, Sue."

He stopped walking and then asked me again, "Sue, you will you be my wife, won't you?"

This time I didn't hesitate. I knew my answer straight away. "Yes, I will," I replied.

"Then no more of this small talk. Let us go and find food from the street sellers. We are weak with hunger, and we need to celebrate and give some food to the gods," said Bunny.

His reply seemed strange to me, as I wouldn't call a wedding acceptance "small talk," but I knew he didn't mean it like that; it was just the way it sounded. I didn't understand about giving food to the gods yet, but I guess this was all a part of the new life I was about to take on.

I found out later that it's the custom with Traditionalists where they give the first mouthful of food to the gods to thank them. Then they begin to eat.

We spent many days talking and learning about each other's cultures over the next few weeks. I felt ready to move to Nigeria to meet his family. Also, I realised this was expected of me. We had also planned to marry there, so my life was very quickly changing, and each day I could feel myself falling head over heels in love with this spellbinding person. We had decided to get the money together and fly to Nigeria to get married as soon as possible. This involved me getting some money sent from England to enable us to hurry the process up, as we were not earning very much at all in the Gambia and needed money for our tickets to fly. The flight, I learned, would take around six hours from Banjul. Bunny decided that he would surprise his father by just appearing back home with his bride from England. It all sounded very romantic, but we needed to get through all the complicated logistics of getting there first.

Love
*And love took a hold*
*Into the blood, mind, heart, bodies*
*Lying on the bed waiting for him*
*Lips, hands, bodies, souls entwined.*
*As into each other we moved*
*In, out, around we go together*
*Black as the night, against a white body*
*The rhythm of our sexual dance began.*
*African large, strong lips kissed mine*
*Dreadlocks draped over my body*
*Sweating in the Gambian heat,*
*We were now truly united.*
*Love had found us wanting,*
*Our lives were now renewed.*

# CHAPTER 10

# HARD TIMES IN BAKAU

January 1997 in the Gambia. Only this time last year I thought, I was there on holiday. Wow, how my life has changed in a year. But now the winter season was upon us, and there was a definite chill in the air. The marketplace near where Bunny and I lived had all been uprooted. It was now a sea of rusty nails and old pieces of wood, like a shanty town. Heaps of stale vegetables surrounded the debris. Things were changing around us, but the changes that we required were not fast enough. There were changes in the compound too; my neighbours had started stealing some of my possessions. I had started to separate myself from the women a little where I lived, owing to the fact that one of the women had stolen my skirt off the washing line and had the nerve to wear it in the main house of Mama N'jie. I felt sick that they would do that, then when I began to examine the rest of my washing, I noticed some of my towels were missing. I questioned each of them about my new missing towel that had been sent to me from England, but they all denied it and suggested perhaps someone had come into the compound and stolen it off the line. Gradually, I could see all the items I had arrived with going missing. A sort of silent ongoing theft was occurring. It felt as though as long as I was nice, friendly, and kind to everyone, they would feel it was their right to beg, steal, or borrow anything I had.

A friend of mine, Pauline, an expatriate who had been living in the Gambia had told me not to live too close to the Gambians who were poor, as they would want everything I had. If I wasn't careful, I would soon be living out of a small holdall with no luggage and no luxuries.

I think I felt worse about my poverty because I'd discovered that many of the aid workers who came into Banjul via established charity links were provided with good accommodation and had all their food provided, plus assistance in settling into their work, as part of their package. I'd met a few charity workers eating and drinking in some of the nice hotels on my first night in Africa when Mass and Momodu showed me round. However, as I came to the Gambia as an independent worker with a poor African charity and was not on a fixed contract with a British company, these luxuries weren't available to me. Looking at it positively, it meant I was experiencing true life in Africa, which is why I had made close friends with some of the Africans, as, like them, sometimes I too needed food and shelter with very little money.

Still I had good health, and I was so in love. So, I tried to put these worries aside. The compound continued to be busy with the women working in the streets, busy selling corn or working at night trading. There were two young boys who ran around the compound in the afternoons. Even though they had very few toys to play with, they seemed so happy. I began to think they were happy in their innocence. They'd never experienced the wealth of a first-world country, so they were blissfully ignorant about their lack of toys, phones, or high-tech equipment. They were happy to just be and play with bits of wood and cardboard boxes. A new bicycle arrived one day, and it was a sheer joy to these boys.

Every morning during the rush hour, all I seemed to see was hectic traffic, red dust, pollution, happy high-life music, noisy people, and beggars; yet at other times of the day, the sandy streets of the capital, Banjul, felt more like a village than a city. It's dominated by Arch 22, named after the military takeover here on July 22nd 1994.

In the middle of Gambia, the centre is the busy and chaotic trading place named Royal Albert Market, where peanut grinders, wig makers, fabric printers, and everyone in between, gather in alleyways that wind down to the shore of the river.

I loved seeing the children walk down the streets in their beautifully coloured school uniforms. This was one discipline that had been continued by the Gambians after being ruled by the British for over thirty-nine years.

However, not all children got to go to school, as schooling wasn't free. In Gambia, and the parents have to pay for school fees. Many children who were part of the Schools for Progress charity received donations sent from all over the globe, which paid for their schooling.

# CHAPTER 11

# THE DISAPPEARING FLIGHT TICKETS

DHL office, first stop Banjul—there, it was clearly written on my list of things to do. I disembarked from the bus after a twenty-minute journey from Bakau. Today was January 25th 1997, a big day with lots of things to do to start our departure, hopefully, from the Gambia. The sun shone brightly in Banjul. As usual, beggars called after me shouting "Irelyate!" when I passed them, which loosely interpreted in English means "charity." I knew that I couldn't spare them even one dalasi today. Usually if I had some spare change, I would give it, but I was not so flushed with money now. Every pound of my savings of £500 was allocated to our escape from the restrictions of the Gambia. It seemed the more I spoke to people about visiting the Gambia, the more I kept hearing that it's easy to get in, but it can be difficult to leave, especially if you come to work as a charity worker, as you will then not earn any money. So, you will find it hard to save enough cash to fly out.

Even though I was working—due to the exchange rate there—when you consider your wages and look at the exchange rate, it was not enough, and having Mom's money from my savings was a godsend, as it gave us some English currency, which we could use to buy our flight tickets and maybe even have a little bit to spare.

I arrived at the DHL office to see two friendly girls dressed in their smart red-and-white uniforms. So, I greeted them and asked for the recorded delivery envelope from my Mother. After I'd shown them my identity card and my passport then they handed me the package when I opened it, there was a little card wishing me well and the cheque I needed to give Globe Travel for our flight tickets out of Gambia. I really hoped Mom had spelled *Globe* correctly on the cheque, as she had received the information down a crackly telephone line from when I phoned her in the middle of a busy traffic area near Gamtel's office. I was glad it was all happening—phew! It was OK. We were going to eat now we had some money at least. We had been living on bread and mayonnaise for days.

Next on the list was a visit to Globe Travel in Buckle Street. You may well ask what she is doing with a cheque but we did not have any guaranteed way in the 1990's in West Africa to receive money quickly.

I rushed past the newspaper office where I had previously worked and spared a little thought for my co-workers working hard on a boiling hot Saturday morning to publish the *Gambia Daily*. I heard from one of my ex-members of staff that it had suffered a bad week as the army had arrested the editor and stuck him in jail for twenty-four hours. The president, I heard, had objected to an article he had written; it was undiplomatic apparently. I thought, I am living in very scary times. What had happened to the freedom of the press? I needed to now wake up and understand that this was not the UK. I wondered about the principles I had been taught of legal, honest, and decent stories in journalism and if these applied there. It was not like the UK or United States, where one could sue the press. Especially if the president owned the paper you were working on. So, I had a lot to learn and I felt it was time for me to leave and start my married life.

By 10:20 a.m. I was sitting at the counter in the Globe Travel office, in front of Mr. Cham, Mr N'jie's assistant, who informed me there were two seats available for tomorrow. Tomorrow, tomorrow, I kept saying to myself. I couldn't wait to rush back to the compound to inform Bunny. Then we'd have to quickly pack! And I still had to buy a typewriter ribbon for the word processor in order that I could type the letter listing my charitable goods for customs. These included a large old TV of my own that the charity did not want, and also, I had some books I had purchased in the Gambia for children, and of course my typewriter. Gosh, there was so much to do! We'd probably be packing well into the night. And then there was Mama N'jie's rent to sort out. My mind whizzed through the rest of our list of things to do.

The travel agent, Mr Cham, idly thumbed through the precious tickets. Our method of escape just sat there waiting on the desk for us. The fan above my head clanged loudly. I tried to distract my thoughts by watching people come into that office from the main street. Everyone seemed so happy and spent a long time greeting each other in typical Wolof friendly manner. Many of the shop visitors—those lucky enough to have enough money—were bound for Mecca on the Muslim pilgrimage. I had to wait as Mr. Cham said he needed to check the confirmation number from Ghana Airways. But forty minutes later, I was still waiting, so I decided to read Mom's note. I could handle it now. I always had to psyche myself up to read the letters from my mom, as I always felt tearful when I saw her handwriting because I missed her so badly. I was now ready. I could handle it. It confirmed the enclosed cheques—one for Globe and two made out to me for one hundred pounds each from her personally. She finished the note by wishing Bunny and me "a happy life." Life! It all seemed so final. A long and happy *life* I hadn't really thought it in terms of a *life*…Then a final note about the family sending me all their love. I bit back the tears as Mom's face loomed large in my imagination. I knew my mother loved me unconditionally. I would miss her, well, everyone, so much. But now it was time for action.

I asked to see the boss himself personally, and I was invited into Mr Cham's private office. He introduced me to his wife, who was dressed expensively in beautiful embossed Dakar printed material with an enormous head-dress and bedecked with Egyptian-style gold jewellery with Arabic rings.

I felt her eyes look me up and down. It was obvious sometimes that some wives do not accept a single woman when their husband is doing business with her in Africa, especially if the woman is a young or younger British lady. She continued sizing me up.

As far as she could see, I was a white lady who was getting special treatment from her husband over and above the call of duty. She did not respect that Mr N'jie and I had worked together to organise all the promotions he ran on the radio and in the newspaper to help their business to sell the tickets. This profit that bought her those lovely items of clothes and jewellery.

She glanced down at my short dress and bare brown legs. I saw a small frown appear over her eyes. A Muslim woman never shows her legs, so we had cultural differences too. I wished that I had dressed less seductively that day. My spotted sundress was very pretty, but not at all African style. Her mouth smiled as she greeted me, but her eyes were cold and unkind as we eyed each other for a few seconds.

Around his office placed in high piles were tickets, visas, and passports for the pilgrims going on the trip he'd organised. He had conjunctivitis in his left eye and bathed it constantly. I asked him what the delay was and why he had not given me my tickets. Why had he still not processed Mom's cheque and given me my tickets? He did look anxious and stressed out. He walked to the main desk, and his wife followed behind him. He spoke in Wolof to her about me for a few seconds; then, she turned to me and said, "We cannot accept that cheque. It must be cash only for the tickets."

The words stung. I was speechless. Then, Mr. N'jie followed the devastating news by saying, "And anyway, I have no tickets or money left. All business is allocated to the hajj trip (Mecca) and Umra (holy place of worship). Sorry."

*Sorry*—what kind of word was that? I've always felt that it was a small word, too easy to say, and I felt this even more since visiting Africa. Man does terrible atrocities and says sorry. Does it replace the severed head or arm in battle? Does it mend the broken heart? Bunny once warned me how Africans can lead you on and then disappoint you at the very last moment. He mentioned that always they can tell you yes instead of being straight with you in the beginning. At that time, I disagreed with him, calling him cynical, but he said he knew his fellow men better than I. Bunny seemed to know his fellow men better than I. He was right; he did. But that didn't matter now. All I knew then was that the travel agent had disappointed me twenty-four hours before my flight was due.

I cupped my face in my hands. Should I cry? No, I would make him feel terribly guilty. Instead, I took the angle of the distressed victim. I was one after all.

The flight cheque my mother had so lovingly sent, which had cost her thirty-six pounds via DHL, lay useless on his polished fake-wood-laminated desk. I gathered my belongings and left without saying goodbye and with my head held high. I ran to two more travel agents, presenting the cheque and begging to travel with them, but to no avail. Only hard cash talks in Africa. No one trusts foreigners with cheques buying single tickets out of their country.

I ran to the street boys, the professional money changers, and presented the two other cheques for one hundred pounds each. I worked out that would give me 300 dalasi's, and I thought maybe I could beg or borrow the rest. I was obsessed with flying out now. Never before had I verbally booked a seat on a plane and not flown; it would be unheard of in England. However, not even the street boys who changed money would accept a cheque as it was crossed. I guess I should have known better. I had changed enough money on the black market before I had a bank account there in Gambia to know all this. I was getting desperate. I was running around in circles.

At 1:50 p.m., ten minutes before they would all close their offices, I had one last try and asked Mr Darboe, the man on the desk at Ghana Airways, what I should do. He looked sympathetic but couldn't help.

"I'll be at the airport tomorrow, if you want to pay then. Otherwise, you could try the British embassy—see if they can help you? Good luck!" he said.

I travelled home, totally dejected and completely in shock. Bunny and I would be left behind there. When I told Bunny, he said, "It was not our time." He said it to reassure me but wasn't really much comfort. It seemed we needed to suffer a while longer before we could travel to Agbor, Bunny's hometown in Delta State, Nigeria.

Fortunately, that weekend Bunny and I were delighted not to have another weekend of actually starving. The Sky Juice Band had just been paid for a gig, so we could go out and buy our own food instead of eating food from the street sellers.

The sponge mattress, which we had on the floor for sleeping on, was getting a bit worn, and it seemed to hold the moisture around your body, which was quite uncomfortable for me. At night as I lay awake sometimes, in the distance, I could hear the entertainment in the hotels, drumming to amuse the holidaymakers. I'd also occasionally hear taxis rolling up outside, dropping people off in the marketplace. And some nights, I could hear a crunching noise as my neighbour killed the cockroaches that would come out at night and move across the floor in his room. He would kill them by smacking down hard on the floor with his flip-flop as they scurried across the floor. But most nights we just seemed to curl up together and forget our hardship. If I could not sleep, I would get up and write poems about my feelings and noises I heard or just about our situation.

We had a massive plan to go to Nigeria and marry, and nothing else mattered.

Next day there was a loud knock on the iron gates of the compound; it was Omar from the newspaper office, holding a plastic container of milk that he'd brought from his father's cow. At least I could enjoy the taste of fresh milk again whilst staying in the compound. I woke Bunny, who was dozing in the heat.

"Bunny, it's Omar at the gate. I am going out to collect some milk. I can see him holding it up. Look!"

Bunny peered through the curtain at my window, not impressed at being woken up.

"Why is this milk so important? I never drink that stuff."

"Well, I do, and it's difficult to give it up, Bun."

I wrapped a cotton cloth around my body and tied it over my breast and ran to the gate to thank Omar for such a gift. I knew he had carried that milk a long way across Gambia to bring to my gate.

"Thank you, Omar. It's very much appreciated."

"It is no problem, Suzanne. I got it from my brother's house in Barra. I went by boat on my day off to see him, and he has a cow."

"How much money is it?"

"It is a gift from my family to you and Bunny. Goodnight, miss. I need to go back. It is getting late."

I bade him goodbye and carried the milk to Mama N'jie's main house and placed it on the shelf of the fridge in her kitchen. Then I returned to bed, feeling very impressed that a member of my staff was now becoming a friend.

Bunny had fallen asleep when I returned to my bed, and I sat trying to think of how I could perhaps in the future promote Omar by speaking to my ex-boss, as he was learning very fast and seemed very ambitious.

I lay listening to the ladies moving around the compound and putting their children to bed and lighting their kerosene lamps in the darkness. I heard a child being scolded and wrote this poem quickly as it came into my head.

Poem
*The smack in Mama N'jie's compound.*

*The cracking noises*
*The screaming boy*
*Shouts, "Why, why, why?"*
*Loud, into the darkness of our compound*

*I want to rush in to stop this*
*Memories haunt me*
*My own childhood remembered*
*The helplessness felt then*

*Pain across his poor legs*
*Loud screams continue from the boy*
*A lady from Senegal, our visitor*
*Rushes in to rescue this violent scene*

SUE HADLEY

*The boy races to his hut*
*His brother waits there*
*A silent sadness prevails*
*Another child's pillowcase lies wet*

*Tomorrow, family life assumes shape*
*In the net of our compound*
*Before the call of Allah in Africa.*

# CHAPTER 12

# BRITISH EMBASSY TO THE RESCUE

The only good thing that had come out of that very frustrating Globe Travel cock-up, I reckoned, was Mr Darboe's advice— "Why not try the British embassy?"

Bunny and I rose early and got to the British embassy by 9:30 a.m. It was a beautiful building, only a mile or so away, set in nice gardens along Atlantic Road, Fajara. The guard at the gate gave Bunny a badge as he wasn't British. We walked through the gardens to the main building, both wondering how long it would be before we could fly to Bunny's home.

At the front desk, the Gambian secretary asked if she could help us.

"Yes, can I help you?"

"Err, yes. I'd like to see someone personally please."

"What is it about?" she replied.

"Well, it's a monetary matter actually."

"Yes, but what is it about?" she inquired yet again.

Trust me to get a nosy one, I thought.

"I'm having trouble getting some money into the country."

"Go through the next door," she advised.

Bunny and I walked through the next door. That door felt like our last hope. There were large posters around the room of London and Oxfordshire's Blenheim Palace in England. Bunny started asking me questions about the place, so I pointed out the Thames, Buckingham Palace, and other places and told Bunny I'd take him sightseeing in London and Oxford one day. Bunny said he thought London looked a bit like Lagos, because they also have many big buildings like that. He really loved the beauty of England and looked forward to perhaps one day getting there as my husband.

"That's Buckingham Palace, is it?"

"Yes," I said. "I'll take you there one day." I looked through the glass panel. The room was laid out like a bank with smoked glass placed high around it so that you couldn't get in. A blond British boy was on the computer. He seemed friendly enough. Soon, an official approached and introduced himself as Mr Chadmore and let us into his office. As he was quite a rotund man, sporting a dark-brown beard, I thought he looked more like a boy-scout master than an embassy official. He listened quickly and then asked how I was managing at present. I showed him my mother's cheques; my spirits lifted, but I was afraid to get too excited after yesterday's disappointment. He came back several minutes later with the bad news that the method wouldn't work, as it has to be a personal cheque with a cheque guarantee card, plus they couldn't change such a large amount as £500.

Just as I thought we'd come to another dead end, he said, "But we do transfers."

"Do you? How does that work?"

"Your mother phones this number and speaks to a lady named Claire in London. Then we receive the money from there."

I couldn't believe it. Now I needed to speak to Mom urgently. It was ten thirty now, Gambian time. That's about one hour behind English time, so Mom would be at her office for the next half an hour. I asked Mr Chadmore if I could phone from his office. He agreed.

I quickly picked up the handset and dialled Mom's work number. "Is that BR Plastics?"

"Yes."

"Hello, can I speak to Celia please?"

"Yes, just a minute," the receptionist answered in her British accent before asking me who she could say was calling.

"Can you tell Celia it's her daughter Sue in Africa, please?"

I heard the receptionist there call my mother to the phone.

"Hello, Sue," my mom answered in an emotional voice.

"Hi, Mom," I replied in a very excited voice.

"Did you get my cheques?"

"Yes, Mom, but I can't use them because they don't accept that system anymore."

"Oh dear," she said, sounding upset. "What can I do now, Sue?"

I told her I was at the British embassy in the Gambia with a man named Mr. Chadmore and gave all the details. Mother rushed for a pen and said she would help. I passed the phone to the gentleman, and they spoke briefly. I could tell Mom had won him over with her charming telephone manners. I wasn't surprised. I don't know anyone who dislikes my mom. She is by nature friendly and very efficient. The official smiled and seemed to have dropped his "stiff upper lip" a little. He passed me the phone to say my goodbyes. I heard myself say, "Miss you, Mummy." I was full of emotion.

"Miss you too, darling." I heard her say before the call ended.

Mr Chadmore then said, "Now, you need to give me the phone number of your compound. Then we will contact you in a couple of days. OK?"

I thought, Two or three days' time, wow! I suppose if Mom pays that method on her card it could well be that fast.

I inquired, "How much does it cost for a transfer then?"

"About twenty-eight pounds or so," Mr. Chadmore replied.

"Oh, right, thanks, look forward to hearing from you. I will give you the telephone number at our compound, and perhaps you can let me know as soon as possible then?"

I shook his hand and said I'd await his call. True to his word, by Wednesday at 4:30 p.m. he'd phoned the compound and asked me to call the very next day, as they'd have cashed the cheque for £600. Wow! One hundred pounds more than anticipated. Good old Mom.

That night I couldn't sleep and wrote another of my poems about Bunny.

*African Lover and Husband*
*A stranger from Africa*
*Bunny Rasta, a prince and chief priest*
*My heart too long had waited*
*Now love had arrived*
*On my African doorstep*
*My soulmate—two old souls*
*In perfect loving harmony*
*Into the eternity of love's path*
*Casting me adrift from Western ways*
*Love, just like a visitor that never leaves,*
*Stays on well into the night's darkness*
*Reaching within private, deep thoughts.*
*Love, all-consuming now, no boundaries*
*Your black ebony body shining against my white skin*
*Absorbing my body and soul*
*Walking, talking, loving, and sleeping*
*In each other's company, daily*
*Discussing reincarnation together*
*Had we found each other anew?*
*We seemed to already know each other*
*Had all our past yearnings come to this?*
*Destined to be as one*
*Love led us to stay together*
*Considering another's views*
*My twin soul resonating*
*Influencing entrancing bewitched.*

CHAPTER 13

# IN TRANSIT

It was now February 2nd and we had many hours of travelling ahead of us to get us from Banjul, the capital of the Gambia, to Nigeria. We were up at 5:00 a.m. that Sunday in Bakau.

The packing was more or less completed—all except the toiletries, so we had six items of luggage on the floor in our room, waiting to go to new homes. What we couldn't or didn't want to take with us, we'd tried to find homes for, so for example our fan was going to one of Bunny's band members.

Amazingly for that time in a morning, we weren't the only ones up! N'gormy, my lady friend from the compound, was up and about. As a strict Muslim, she was always up to pray early at the call of Allah. N'gormy was a Jola tribeswoman who did a little cleaning job half of the day and then spent the rest of the day selling ice creams to the children who would call at the compound to buy from her. I'd never seen her with a husband, so she worked hard whilst doing her best to bring her daughter's three boys up whilst the daughter lived in America.

I knocked on her door and gave her my spare toiletries and a large towel, and she hugged me goodbye.

"Please give Mama N'jie this key to my hut, would you?" I asked.

She nodded and looked sad to see me leave. I would miss them all in our compound, but I was excited about how things would be different now that I was to marry Bunny.

We just had time to shower, eat our meagre scraps of food, and pack the last few things before the taxi arrived.

It was just 6:25 a.m. when we loaded the luggage into the old taxi—as well as our suitcases and charity items and my treasured word processor. Unsurprisingly, we were well over our luggage allowances; in fact, our excess luggage alone weighed twenty-eight kilos. We purchased two tickets via Ghana Airways; then after a two-hour wait, we boarded the plane. So, finally on that plane, I thought, we could begin our exciting journey to our new lives in Nigeria.

Once on the plane, the early start caught up with me, and I nodded off, shortly to be awoken with a nudge from Bunny.

"Wake up, Sue. We have to get off the plane here in Ghana because of fog and mist."

I could not believe what I was hearing! We were to land in Ghana for the evening due to bad weather.

So, we finished up sitting in the Kotoka International Airport, surrounded by all our luggage. The Gambia airline had to give us accommodation, and we were delighted to be allocated a room in the Mariset Hotel in Ghana. Bunny had never seen a hotel so fantastic and couldn't believe we were going to sleep there for free!

There were several of us who waited outside the hotel very early the next morning for our lift to the airport to resume our journey. We all stood waiting, with sleep still in our eyes, as the sun shone down on us in Ghana, until the small bus arrived to take us back to the airport. We had to battle again with our luggage, not helped by the fact that the conveyor belt wasn't working. Then finally we flew to Lagos airport. The whole journey from Gambia to Nigeria had taken us twenty-four hours. Bunny noted that the air time from Gambia normally would have been just a six-hour flight. Six-hour flight, I thought? Africa is enormous! It took me six hours to fly from London to Gambia and now another six hours across Africa to reach Nigeria. This is amazing!

The journey had by no means finished, as we were then to travel over five hours by road from Lagos to Agbor in Delta State, Nigeria.

# CHAPTER 14

# LAGOS ARRIVAL

I feel Lagos has to be experienced by any traveller. The culture shock is unbelievable as the dust and dryness just hits you. I have never heard such noise or seen so many people constantly move about! A hot, dusty sprawling city with a population that Bunny estimated in 1997 was probably up to thirteen million. It was one of the fastest growing cities in the world, it felt like an overcrowded, heaving, and poverty-stricken crazily busy and bustling city. The constant movement of people daily has to be experienced. The dust and dryness hit me. We had been travelling almost two days. The traffic jams along the major roads and bridges gave beggars and peddlers a chance to sell their wares. You can buy anything from fruit, eggs, and peanuts to batteries and watches.

The street boys and girls with such pleading eyes hit you as they shout and beg at your car window; it is really scary when you first experience it. They are very cheeky and really know how to just look at you so that you feel guilty. It makes you feel such pity for them struggling to make a living. The little girls often just wear flip-flops and dirty dresses. The young men are dressed in their dirty shirts, designer fake watches, and trainers. A complete contrast to the businessmen in their shiny suits and nylon shirts with leather shoes and a mix of Muslim attire too. It makes a fascinating contrast. The vivid array of women wearing brightly coloured cotton tops who sit or stand in the marketplace, selling their wares, is something you never forget. The mothers with children call to each other whilst their children run amongst them. Some women lean over their wares with their children strapped to their backs as they shout to sell their spices in the midday sun.

Radios and CD players blast out lively (African high life) style of music as you pass, whilst beggars with deformed legs sit on skates and tug your clothes saying, "Aunty, sister, give me, dash me?" I rarely saw a wheelchair for those poor disabled beggars. I had to turn away because if you're not careful in Lagos, you could easily give away all your money to beggars.

"Hold your purse well," Bunny shouted as we moved amongst people in the streets.

"OK, I will," I replied.

I checked again to see if my money was well hidden around my waist in my money belt. Although, to be honest, there was not much money left.

Whilst my senses were trying to take in everything that was going on around me, I also had to try to concentrate to as stop myself falling in the massive ditches in the road and to avoid all the people who were everywhere, especially under the bridges, where they seemed to trade and sleep. They lived in absolute squalor.

We stopped for hot pepper soup and watched the boys who were trying to make money cleaning shoes. They were chasing everyone they could, even people in suede desert boots (like me) to persuade them to have their shoes cleaned by looking up at them with pleading eyes. Really, it's hard to hold back your feelings; you have to and maybe just give a few naira's away to have your shoes cleaned as this was their way of life as street children there.

We'd been travelling for two days now, and we were exhausted, hungry, and thirsty. Ahead of us was a large bridge that we had to use to cross over the road, with large steel steps. I really wasn't sure I had the energy to get across that with all our belongings, but I could see Bunny ahead of me with a case on top of his head, walking up those steps as though it was no weight at all. It gave me the strength I needed to start carting all our boxes and bin bags over it to the other side of the bridge. I managed those steps as if my life depended on it, which I guess in some way it did!

A yellow battered transit van, I guess the local bus service, trundled past us with people packed in like sardines. The local bus service, I gathered. People were staring and commenting on my hair. Most expats living there seemed to have government jobs and moved around in air-conditioned cars, except poor travellers like me with no car. The sweat trickled down my back, and a burning desire to pee and drink tons of water hit me. I was dehydrating, and yet the heat still soared. The noise of the constant beeping of car horns and large trucks thundering by plus people talking and shouting was deafening. I wondered if somehow the Lagosian just didn't hear the noise anymore, and whether I'd eventually be able to drown it out too.

I kept my eyes ahead as Bunny carried my case on his head. I struggled with our two boxes for charity and hand luggage. It was a far cry from the college job I had left in the UK it seemed.

We finally arrived at the taxi area, where Bunny spent the next ten minutes haggling for a good fee to Agbor by taxi.

Meanwhile, I had to stay out of sight, as Bunny said if the driver saw a white woman or should I say an *oyinbo* (white woman) with heavy luggage, the price would go up. Little did I know that I would travel for over six hours in that cab to a new dusty home.

Bridge in Lagos

# CHAPTER 15

# AGBOR COMPOUND

The old battered yellow taxi clanged along through all the towns. The suspension seemed to have gone, and I could feel the springs pushing the through the seats. It was to be several hours of an exhaustingly hot journey.

After an hour or so, Bunny turned and said "Sue, where is the ghetto blaster? I want to put some batteries in it so that we can hear our tapes."

"Isn't it in the boot, Bun?"

Bunny suddenly looked shocked as he replied,

"*OH*, hell no. I didn't see it when we loaded up in Lagos."

My mouth dropped open as I said," You had it on the plane in your hand luggage. Then I saw you carrying it off the plane."

"Oh no, I put it down when we were collecting all the luggage off the conveyor belt. Someone must have stolen it then."

Bunny asked the driver to stop the car whilst we searched the boot, but we both knew the truth that my ghetto blaster, stereo centre, had gone.

"Maybe we can phone the airport and report the loss. Perhaps someone will hand it in," I said.

Bunny frowned and replied, "Sue, no-one will hand that in. This is Africa. It's probably in someone's house or being sold already as we speak."

This loss was a very big thing for Bunny as the tape of his band Sky Juice was in it, and it was his last one. It was a loss for me too, as I loved hearing his music and the news on the BBC channel, using the radio facility. In the Gambia, it had kept us abreast of worldly affairs. So, I realised it was a double loss for us that day. I was upset but not as upset as Bunny.

I just thought, It's no problem. We can always get another as soon when we start earning. This was another difference I noticed between Bunny's life and mine. In England material things are often replaceable, as we have insurance, and if not, we earn the money to buy a replacement. But there in Agbor, in a third-world country, it was to be so different. I was to learn many things.

I was to learn there was great poverty amongst the people there. And, I would soon start to really value my money, food, and belongings and really use my education skills if I was to eat well and accomplish my dream of completing this book.

As we drove down the dusty street towards Agbor, I looked out at the ramshackle tin roofs and squalor of refuse in the streets and chickens and goats and wild pigs moving walking loose in the streets, and I wondered how the people ever managed to stay healthy. This was such a shock from the Gambia with its cleaner streets, beautiful buildings, sandy beaches, and hospitality. There were children running down the street shouting, churches everywhere, and people rushing around going about their business in Nigeria and the people looked so happy, maybe I was painting to bad a picture, but this disappointment was planted in my heart. I thought about our finances and started worrying about how I could earn a living there. The business woman in me was beginning to worry. But the artist within me loved the environment for its craziness, and after all, I was to marry a prince, chief priest of Illah; my prince had come to whisk me away from it all!

My brain kicked in and said, I could go freelance surely—perhaps start running some courses in media or counselling there in Abgor or Benin, as both these towns looked busy. But I kept thinking of how poor the people looked and would they be able to afford the training and education?

Maybe there was a library or a university, where perhaps I could go to the library and compose a course. Or maybe I needed to sit down in Africa, as Bunny would say, and think about other skills I may have that could help his people and help us out too. Bunny gazed out of the taxi window in silence, and I felt guilty for perhaps not checking all the luggage again when unloading the items off the conveyor belt. The driver started to chat with Bunny as he needed more petrol and wanted to check the tyres over before we continued. The tyres in Nigeria take a constant pounding as the roads are so rough. We pulled over at a local station and queued with many other cars for petrol. I asked Bunny to speak to a local girl there at the station so that she could direct me to the ladies' toilet.

I approached a very smelly area with very run-down toilets. There was a young girl there with a broom.

"One or two?" shouted the girl to me as I arrived inside the toilet area.

"What?" I said.

"Are you doing a number one or two?"

"Err. A number one. I am going to urinate."

"Then use that one, not this one," she said.

I gathered that the other toilet was broken, and this was her way of dealing with the cleaning. Even if it was broken, it seemed a very private question to me. I laughed as I sat on that smelly, battered toilet. Perhaps the girls asked that question all day as they struggled to keep those toilets unblocked. I was surprised and amused. No secrets here then, I thought. I ran back to the car as the driver in his brightly checked shirt was shouting to his fellow taxi drivers and joking loudly. He seemed to be boasting that he had a good booking. Bunny was annoyed as he was drawing attention to us and already we had lost the music centre. But I liked that driver; he was jolly and hardworking. He told me that he was a Yoruba man and that most of the taxi drivers in Lagos were Yoruba. He seemed chatty, and for a five-hour journey, I suppose he had to try and get to know his passengers.

Finally, four or five hours later, the loud-mouthed driver pulled into the large red dusty drive of Bunny's compound at 48 Umudein Street, Agbor. His stepsister Ifeyinwa ran out to greet us, shouting joyously and jumping up and down. She was a small-framed young girl around eighteen or nineteen years of age and stood next to a little black girl of around twelve years of age in a dress with checks on a smocking across the chest. Both had braided black thick hair which was tied back and wore flip-flops.

They ran around us and hurried to help us get our luggage out of the car whilst Bunny settled the bill with the driver and offered him a drink of water before he made his way off out of the compound. He said he needed to get back before it got dark as no one wants to drive in the dark. I was surprised at the comment. I did not know then that there were very few streetlights, and often people would get robbed by highway robbers with guns if they were unlucky.

This was all new to me. But I was happy to have arrived and looked around the dusty square of the compound at a large red-brick sandy building and several small huts placed around a courtyard with a totem pole. We were to stay in the small houses on the left as you arrived into the compound as Bunny had built that and felt it was private to begin our new life. It needed a good coat of paint and a sweep through as it had been empty a while, Bunny mentioned as we sat on the old rusty bed with a spring base. I loved it as it was our first home, and I really liked the idea of getting it painted and making do.

The girls ran around and started cooking whilst Bunny and I rested on the bed.

When I awoke two hours later, Ifeyinwa, my sister-in-law-to-be, said, "What is your name?"

"Suzanne, and yours?"

"Ifeyinwa. Are you his concubine or his wife?"

"What? Oh, I am his wife-to-be. We will marry very soon."

"That is a great thing. Then we will be relatives, won't we?"

"Err, yes, I suppose so. Where do you live?"

She grabbed my hand and led me around the compound yard and through the main house to show me her two rooms where she lived with her mother and Mercy, the little girl. There was no kitchen and no running water in that house and very little electricity, and they cooked in the yard over wood and bamboo fires, squatting over them, fanning the smoke. It was a relatively poor household but clean. In the corner of the yard, there was a small garden area with banana plants and a couple of sheds—one was for showering and one was the communal toilet. Bunny was busy arranging for tables and chairs from the huts in the yard to be dusted down and brought to our new little house.

There were no sofas or comfy chairs, and our second-hand, old TV refused to work as hard as we tried to fix it. It was to be a very primitive life for me, but I was in love, so I didn't care. I had not had running water or air conditioning in Gambia, so I was becoming African already. Bunny was sending messages out to workmen to come and fix the ceiling fans in our house so that I could cope with the heat. Later that day, he also chatted to two painters to employ them to come and see the work they were to do in the next few days to make the place habitable. We were to have white gloss paint to cover the rusty railings that surrounded the house, and all the window frames were to be painted. The walls were to be a pale blue.

Everyone in the compound seemed to be sweeping before the light faded, and a pitch-black Nigerian night came upon us. I was to develop an African eye if I was to walk out of the compound at night, and also Bunny would not let that happen until we had a torch that worked and until Oney, his brother, arrived to be my escort. I was to discover that my freedom would be limited as Nigeria at that time was a dangerous place to be alone in at night. It was to be very different from all the freedom I had experienced in the Gambia, which was busy with tourists of all creed and colour.

The next morning, we ate rice and a tomato-and-fish sauce, and as we were taking our showers, I heard a loud voice in the yard and saw Bunny running to meet Onochie, who was the youngest of Bunny's brothers. He was a tall, handsome Nigerian with a beautiful voice, and he was built like a boxer. He had massive muscles on his arms, and he wore a white T-shirt and jeans and rubber flip-flops. He was delighted to meet me and spent the day chatting to me and helping me to settle in as Bunny organised the painters, who seemed to splash paint everywhere they went. "Oney," as he preferred to be called, offered to translate when we were in crowds of people and to teach me Igbo, which was a godsend. I found the language difficult as it seemed sounded very nasal. I later discovered we were to settle there for a couple of weeks only, before going to meet his father in Illah to marry.

That day Oney and Bunny decided to walk to Reliance the local quiet area to catch up on the family news.

Bunny & Oney in Reliance, Agbor

# CHAPTER 16

# THE MARRIAGE CEREMONY

Seventh February, this was very special to both Bunny and me. We had decided to marry that month, partly because Bunny, practical as ever, couldn't see the point of hanging around for another week in Illah, "wasting time" as he put it "with unnecessary socialising."

The message had gone out from neighbours and fellow shrine members via the phone, before 9:00 a.m. that morning, to the town of Illah, to instruct all the chiefs to arrive at 10:00 a.m. I was still in a dream state, partly jet lagged and travel weary, stressed out, and shattered from doing two jobs in the Gambia.

"Bunny, I don't have a wedding dress or anything with me," I moaned.

"Look, just wear that dress you have hanging there. You'll look wonderful," he replied. I glanced across the bedroom of Bunny's house in Illah at my blue Marks and Spencer sundress.

"It will have to do," I said to myself.

"Maybe we can have another celebration in Agbor with the women there when we get back. I will make sure we buy a new dress there to wear."

I thought of brides in England spending their morning at the hair salon, having beauty treatments done, their hair styled, and nails manicured. But, there's that saying that "in Rome, you have to do as the Romans do," so I pulled out a red-and-blue sarong to brighten the dress up a bit and found a brown ponytail-type hairpiece that I could wear wrapped round my own long hair for volume. It didn't look too bad after all. The wedding photographs would not be up to British standards, but in the villages, they don't bother with all that. Still, I had a decent camera with me, and I'd taught Onochie, how to use it, so we were all set.

We spent the day visiting all Bunny's friends and relatives in the town. We were attracting large crowds wherever we went. Never had a king's son ever married a white lady before in Illah. Bunny informed me that we were making history there that day. In Illah, the main battle I was trying to fight was the battle against the crushing heat. The pores of my skin were working overtime, and my hair felt constantly stuck fast to my head. My make-up was non-existent after half an hour, so eventually I just gave up putting any on. Showering twice, sometimes three times a day seemed to be the only way to cope. It was even hotter than the Gambia there, and I thought that place was hot.

Bunny's family were busy organising all the cooking. A goat and chickens had been slaughtered. Children were busy shouting to each other in the communal kitchen as they took it in turns to pound the yams in front of the house. I picked up Mom's wedding-day card that she had so lovingly sent. "Wishing you happiness in your new life together," it said and was signed "God bless, love, Mom and Dad and the rest of family" along with some kisses. I couldn't stop the tears, which plopped onto the card. The pink flowers it just looked so pretty, like the kind I should have in a bouquet or in my house on my wedding day. I was feeling a little bit sorry for myself, as not even a wedding ring did I possess. I chastised myself and reminded myself that surely it was the actual union of love that mattered, not the dresses or rings. Bunny and I would be together officially. Officially! Panic struck me when I thought I have only known Bunny for ten weeks; this is madness. Also, I don't have my birth certificate, but as no-one had asked me for it so far, I hoped it wasn't necessary, and I tried not to worry myself about all that.

I lay down to rest, but with the heat I quickly fell asleep. I woke up with a start when I heard people starting to arrive. I started to panic and quickly grabbed a towel. Bunny was already on the porch, organising the drinks and a local palm wine to share as this was the tribal custom there in

Nigeria. So, then I rushed to the bathroom to shower with cold water as quickly as possible, very annoyed with myself for falling asleep in the heat and having to rush to get ready on such a special day.

"Oh well, they'll have to take me as I am," I said aloud; then laughed to myself as this was one of my mom's expressions. I wondered whether Mom and Dad were thinking of me at that moment, and Helen and Marian, and all who knew me. I thought, I'm sure if they could see me they would raise a glass to toast me, happy to know I was getting married.

The time difference in Nigeria is that in English summertime, it is the same time. But when we change our clocks in Autumn, then there is one-hour difference. So, the girls could phone me anytime, in reality, but most of the time they called my mother or relied on my letters to know how I was doing. My mother and father had never been to Africa, so I tended to phone Mom and tell her as much as possible when she started asking questions.

Helen and Marian were both single. They hadn't got around to marriage yet, and I was not sure if they were really bothered about marrying at all actually. They were very liberated; both had good jobs and did not rely on a man to look after them. I wondered if they would ever bother?

They had met Bunny when they visited the Gambia on holiday. Only a month before when they had visited me in the Gambia, both had given me a serious talking to. But I was adamant about Bunny, and they were not going to influence me as they had in the past. The usual criteria for potential husbands back home seemed to be, if I could stand the interrogation, it would go along the lines of the following questions, which would need to be answered.

Has he got a good job?

Has he been previously married?

Does he have other wives?

Is he divorced?

Has he got his own house?

Is he about your age?

Well, Bunny couldn't be cloned like all the men in England. He was nothing like anyone else I had ever met in my life.

I felt my tummy turn over as I dressed in my Marks & Spencer dress, made my hair look pretty, then took a final look in the mirror. I then wished myself good luck and headed outside. Bunny was already outside on that porch, organising the drinks and the local palm wine. (Palm wine is tapped from the palm trees; it resembles wallpaper paste and is very potent—best drunk in the afternoons.) I stepped onto the porch and glanced at Bunny. His eyes sparkled as he looked at me. I knew everything was going to be fine.

At around 4:00 p.m., the chiefs turned up, ready to marry us. There was much handshaking, and then Bunny pulled me aside into his father's room and said, "I think it's best if I do all the talking as I'm expected to give a speech."

"As if I'd talk much!" I said with a hint of sarcasm, but I don't think Bunny appreciated my attempt at humour at this point. It was the custom that the chief priest should talk to his people, and this was even more important with Bunny having been absent for the last three years.

I glanced round at the chiefs. Some were in formal ceremonial-type outfits with their hats on, and others were in Western-style clothes. It was a strange mishmash of outfits, but all these men were proud of their culture and tradition. I was honoured that they had all come at very short notice to wed us. Bunny stood up to make a short speech to thank them all and to explain where he had been for the past three years. It was very solemn, but he seemed to command their attention. His father, the king (chief priest) for the past thirty-seven years, listened on. I could not understand one word of it, but I watched everyone's faces as they listened. All the chiefs seemed interested, as they stared at this new lady who would eventually be the chief priestess and tribal queen of their religion.

Bunny's uncle got up to thank Bunny and then said that perhaps I would be of help to them when I could speak Igbo; then he said in broken English, "In two years' time, she will be speaking Igbo."

Two years? I was deeply offended. Did he think it would take me that long? Was I an illiterate person? I was fuming under my breath, but I managed to just keep smiling demurely. He said that Bunny was not the first boy to bring a white lady home and often these white women would not let their men visit Nigeria again. That these wives then threatened them with divorce if they should go home. I thought the comment was very negative, but perhaps it was true. The uncle then added that because I had brought Bunny home to marry that perhaps I was not like that. I could imagine a lot of women not liking the dirt and depravation there; perhaps they had been used to finer things and didn't want to give up their current lifestyle.

Someone had been sent with our 400 naira to purchase more beer for the chiefs, who were mixing it all with the local palm wine, which was, to my dismay, being poured from a blue plastic container similar to the ones we used for collecting petrol in England.

Bunny's father was dressed in white robes and this reminded me of Gandhi as he sat amidst the noise quietly and serenely with a contented smile on his face, and his pale eyes seemed to sparkle. He was a worldly, intelligent man who had studied English. We had spent one weekend in the chief's large house, and I had sat on the end of his four-poster bed while he asked many questions about England and my life there. He loved looking at the photographs in my bag of my mother and father. He had chuckled at the mass of white hair my father sported in the photographs.

"You are Bunny's true love and life. You will make a good wife, Suzanne. You must write of my people and our lives," he had said many times, although I was not sure what he meant by that. He confided in me that he had waited a long time for this moment, so he was very happy.

The beer was distributed by Dunme Okaonta, who took it upon himself to be the waiter. The old chief sitting next to me wanted beer, but everyone refused to serve him as they told me it wasn't good for his health. The chief sulked as he was obviously a little put out. He was well into his seventies, I would guess, yet everyone continued to ignore him as he put his glass forward to be filled. I was given palm wine to drink, which was warm, white, and milky. It still reminded me of wallpaper paste, but boy, it was potent.

I started to relax. I was the only woman amongst the chiefs. I realised that I was now married. Bunny's mother had spoken in Igbo on my behalf, as I could not conduct my vows in their language. Bunny told me. I kissed Bunny as we stood up to be clapped and cheered. I may not be rich yet, Mommy, but I'm titled. The woman rushed in with naira, and the music began as the young boys drummed and sang out loud. Everyone was clapping in rhythm, and Bunny stood up to dance with me as everyone proceeded to pin money onto our heads and clothes. They were naira notes, and they were being stuffed everywhere. There seemed to be no signing of official documents at this tribal marriage. But Bunny informed me that he would need to go the office in the town and pay and sign for our wedding documents the next day. I had no wedding ring and no family to watch me dance with my new husband, but I was extremely happy.

Suddenly an argument began, as Dunme Okaonta had hidden a bottle of beer for a secret extra drink under the table, and his brother in the homburg hat had spotted him. They proceeded to have a very heated argument. I thought violence was about to begin, but no, it was a lot of shouting and arm waving by the two brothers, who had fought since childhood.

"Bunny, they are spoiling my wedding," I cried.

"No, it's all part of the wedding! If they don't have an argument, they are not enjoying themselves," replied Bunny.

Okafor Azike, who was next senior to the king, got rather loud and aggressive about the crate of beer not being placed by his feet as he had requested when the king retired to his bed and that they should have moved the beer nearer to him to respect his seniority. I couldn't believe the pettiness of the argument. In fact, I started to laugh at the absurdity of the whole thing. Everyone else decided to laugh along with me at the old chief being so silly. He seemed to get more annoyed at this and decided to take his leave with his bottle of beer under his arm and was cursing them all as he stood up to leave. I handed him his shoes in the middle of his cursing at the other chiefs; he then changed his tone immediately and thanked me humbly in English, bowing slightly. This caused even more laughing by the chiefs. Their humour was unique to them, but I enjoyed sharing it that night.

The evening was joyous and full of merriment. Three more young musicians turned up to sing rap songs before finishing off the last of the gin. Then improvisation on drums began, and everyone sang and danced. The family seemed to be all musically talented. However, Bunny was reserved and introvert. I presumed that he was already beginning to assume the role of future king and chief priest of Illah. It seemed I was going to be the more extrovert out of the two of us. Bunny was extrovert but only in the company of fellow musicians and when he was singing at his live performances. Off stage, he was always the good listener and more spiritually inclined.

I retired to bed exhausted, but happy. Bunny joined me after seeing off all the guests. He lay next to me; we were both still jet lagged. We were beginning married life in Africa.

Kolanuts on wedding day

Bunny and I relaxing in Agbor after the wedding.

Dreadlocks Poem

*Long dreadlocks swept and tied on your head*
*Tall and shiny your long legs, ebony man*
*My white thin body moves around you*
*Age is no barrier now we explore love's depths*

*Full of vitality, royal, and regal in all your dealings*
*Large voluptuous lips, your sweet breath encompasses me*
*I gaze at your profile as you undress in our room*
*Honeymooners moving in the Illah night*

*We slip between the white cotton sheets*
*Our hands scan each other's body, delighting*
*Quietly smothering my moans of delight*
*Your sweat drops onto my chest as you enter me*
*I know now that I am whole, joined in matrimony*
*The light streams through the mosquito-netted window*
*As we whisper love's praises and comfort each other.*

(The next day after chatting to Bunny, I wrote these sitting on the porch.)

Igbo Tribal Kings' Expectations Poem

*A queen to me you shall be*
*Public face to show*
*Quiet, serene, beautiful,*
*No emotional outbursts*
*Intelligent, wise in all things*
*Secrets to share, love unlimited*
*Hierarchy to respect*
*Fifteen chiefs to move amongst*
*Although I am the poorest of kings in my kingdom*
*I am rich with your love for me*
*My greatness you will witness*
*People shall now bow to me UGO*
*Welcome, Mrs. Susan Hadley Ugochukwu Anikwe*
*My life in Delta State Nigeria awaits you*
*Our new wealth shall surely come*
*And properties and our shrines shall abound*
*Rise up and follow me, my wife.*

*Poem*
*Married Life*
*Wife of tribal king's son*
*What do you really see*
*Now you look at me?*
*Yesterday I was single, free*
*White middle class*
*Proud and even sassy*
*Younger now African*
*And hatching a plan*
*I'm married, devoted*
*To just one man*

*Blow out your candles*
*That you hold for me*
*White English men*
*For I'm not free*
*I'm Mrs. Ugochukwu Anikwe*
*That's me*

The next day in Illah, I looked through the mosquito net at what was originally Bunny's but now our bedroom window. It was a hive of activity outside our bedroom in the communal kitchen. Bunny's younger family members were cooking our breakfast of goat's meat. The smell permeated the air as they cooked on open fires. Three mongrel dogs sat near the fires, waiting for the morsels of meat that they were hoping would drop off whilst cooking.

The smell was delicious. Breakfast was fufu and goat in hot, spicy okra sauce.

Fufu is a starchy potato-type mix of yams or other starches and is often served as an accompaniment to meat or vegetable stews and soups in Nigeria and West Africa. You eat it with your right hand; scooping the fufu with your fingers, you roll it into a ball before dipping it into your stew or sauce. It has the texture of English dumplings and is made with cornflour—very tasty and fulfilling, I may add. The children delivered it to our room, and the looks on the little faces showed they were proud to serve their new relative. They giggled as they served us and then hung around to see if their new English sister-in-law would be able to eat it or not. I managed with great difficulty as the fufu had to be rolled in my right hand, not my left, which wasn't easy with me being left handed.

So, this was how it was going to be. Bunny and I would be waited on hand and foot and treated with great reverence. Even my washing would be done for me! At last I would be free to be creative. I could write and do my sculpture unhindered. I was hoping that I could adjust and become integrated to this new way of life. It was going to be weird not being the career woman anymore. The old world I had known was now going to be totally alien to me.

My new world would involve travelling around each of Bunny's shrines with him to keep the community interested in African tribal religion. So, the honeymoon was not long, because within a few days, we were to travel back by taxi to Agbor to Bunny's shrine to begin our married life.

Awucha—Chief Priest

*Ras Bunny Ugochukwu*
*A musician and priest*
*Deliverer of Awucha religion*
*Dressed in your white robes*
*Chalk marks on your brown face*
*Father, who is chief priest and king*

*Born in a shrine in Africa*
*The holiest of places.*
*Inside you dear Bunny*
*Just one minute*
*Give me just one minute*
*Inside your head, Bunny Rasta*

*That I may see what you see*
*Hear what you hear*
*To know, as you gaze at me*
*What you are thinking*
*To see myself through your eyes*
*Experience your inner world*

*And speak to the deities*
*In astral conversation.*
*Visited daily by initiates*
*Mixing your herbs and medicines*
*Ancient spells conducted night and day*
*A healer to many who visit.*

My new life had begun there in Agbor, and most days I coped with all the changes and enjoyed travelling out on foot with Mercy the maid or Onochie to buy food from the local marketplace, but today was going to be very different.

A couple and their baby girl, plus three friends, arrived in the shrine. I recognised the child as it was one of the baby girls that Bunny had prayed for in the shrine. The couple had longed for a baby and had been trying for over seventeen years to no avail, but apparently, they had come to the shrine and prayed, with Bunny as their chief priest, and they had now got a beautiful baby girl. They called it "a baby from the shrine." Such is the belief of Africans that they must pray and slaughter animals to please and feed the gods, who have the power to grant a child.

I looked into the dark shrine and saw two baby chicks being hung up by their little feet onto the thick rope piece that hung over some bottles of healing fluids.

They were still chirp, chirp, chirping. Their mother, the hen, who had been transported in the same plastic bag amongst the kola nuts had now been slaughtered.

Everyone seemed to ignore those fluffy yellow chicks crying as they chatted on. The chicks would be there to die slowly to celebrate this birth it seemed.

I could not look at them in that heat dying. I wanted to cut them down and stop this barbaric act, but who was I to change things? I was alone there, miles away from anywhere, and this tradition was and still is practised by thousands of followers.

If a human child is born after prayer and rituals, and it really happens, and everyone believes this to be, who am I to question this? This is what my husband does. He is from a long line of chief priests and kings, and this is the life Bunny has been trained for since he was seven, working with his father the in the twelve shrines here.

The crowds were gathering, and a big black goat had been led into Bunny's shrine, and I knew his throat would be cut by one of the male assistants. I saw them put salt into the goat's mouth to cleanse him and made my escape.

I ran to my house in the compound and buried my head in the pillow as I heard his first cry, as if the goat was saying, "What is going on here?" followed by a bloodcurdling gurgling sound that I will never ever forget and that sickened me to the core.

I left a note for Bunny in our bedroom and then ran into the street and began walking, not sure where I was going, but just to be anywhere but there. I was still struggling to get over the killing of the animals that were routinely slaughtered right there in that shrine. I still could not bear the noise of the goats bleating their last bleat before their throats were cut. I ran to my room and wrote this note.

> My Dearest Bunny,
>
> *Please forgive me being such a baby, but I am finding it hard to accept the killing of the animals in front of us all. I also heard you say after you'd drank too much native gin last night that you did not want to come to bed with me!*
>
> *I know I am not much fun as I seem to be constantly ill these days, but hey, what's happening to us? I have gone for a walk, without a bodyguard, to think things out. I wonder about this path I have chosen here as the wife of a chief and king, a chief's queen--to--be.*
>
> *I am having grave doubts about us as our differences suddenly seem so apparent. I am not sure I can be of your world here, Bunny, much as I love you. It's all just too barbaric and alien to me.*
>
> *Don't search for me.*
>
> Sue.

Bunny heard I had gone missing and sent Oney to find me and bring me back home. Now I guess that Oney had kind of become my bodyguard as he seemed to escort me everywhere. As the only white lady in the town, they felt I was not safe to be out alone. Delta State in Agbor, Nigeria—a place where your passport is worth more than you.

I was brought back after one hour when Oney found me in the town centre about a mile away. Once in the compound, I sat on the bed, forlorn. Bunny arrived and closed the door. It was time for a heart-to-heart.

"I am sorry for saying that I didn't want to come to bed with you. I had too much gin. You are my pride, my wife, and this was wrong of me," he said.

"Of course, it was. I don't want to be outside drinking that native gin for hours, so I come here to bed, and, Bunny, it's very different. I didn't know Nigeria and this religion would be like this. It's all so, so weird," I replied.

"It is my people's way and has been this way since before the white man came with his Bible in the early nineteen hundred. Very soon, Sue, you will be used to these things and take your place as a diviner, seer, and chief priestess. Don't you know you are a princess to me and all our Awucha people?"

"Oh, Bunny, that's a big thing. I think it's too big for me to take on," I replied.

"Sue, you must grow up very quickly and take your place," said Bunny as he sat and looked at me.

I felt the fear in my heart but knew that Bunny was right. I tried to reason with myself along the lines of, I must turn my head away at such killings. Maybe I could politely go for a walk when those goats cried and then had their throats cut. After all, I thought, I'm not a vegetarian. I do eat meat even there in England. It's just that I've never witnessed the slaughtering of those animals.

"OK," I said, "but I must insist, Bunny, while we are talking of these things, that other things change for example there is no female genital mutilation here, as the women do not want it or need it, so can you tell them all it's changed"

Bunny looked surprised and said, "That is also my wish, and none of these things will occur."

Then, with the heart-to-heart over, it was back to normality.

"Bring some of those yams from under our bed with you when you come out, honey," Bunny brightly said, as he left me so that he could continue to work in his shrine.

So, this was how the pattern was to continue, with Bunny holding dancing and celebrations and healing and conducting rituals several times a week. I had no money left. I had no ticket out of Nigeria. I had bought only a single ticket there, and I had to get real about my situation and adapt. This was African life, and maybe in time other white people may come and live in the village or the towns nearby, and I could find friends or work.

I dried my eyes with my skirt and put on a white top to join in the dancing and celebrations that would begin early that afternoon whilst the yam cooked and the goat was skinned and carried over the hot bamboo fire. But I had to close my eyes again as the liver, heart, and kidneys were offered to us on a plate in the evening as a delicacy. Although these ceremonies were not every day, they still were our African tribal life.

Everyone laughed as I asked not to be given the eyes to eat—yet another custom of tribal life. My mind flashed back to UK, where in the past I had been a vegetarian for over seven years, but now here I was eating meat with them all. And not meat as I knew it. Meat in the UK was always wrapped in polythene or cling film in the supermarket or freshly displayed at a clean butcher's shop, whereas the meat there was often fresh off the bone! It was a strange new world Bunny had brought me into!

At around 8:15 p.m., when I went to wash and change, I had to rush to the toilet next to our room. Oh no, a tummy bug from all the food and dancing in the heat without enough fluids again. I could not leave my room, as the yard where our totem pole and dancing area was nowhere near the toilet!

I wondered what the ladies now thought of me—such a lightweight, unable to go the pace with them all. Was I ever going to fit in now?

Ifeyinwa arrived on my porch to pass me buckets of water and comforted me.

"Suzanne, you are not his concubine. You need to try and fit in here."

"I know I'm not his concubine, Ify, and yes, I will try harder to fit in if I can just stop this tummy bug."

"Take some paracetamols, and do not eat old rice, and take rest now," she said, as she disappeared with her torch across the compound to sleep in the hut with her mother. When I was alone in the room later, I reached into my old green holdall to find two anti-diarrhoea tablets; much as I believed many things and admired some of the tribal customs, I still went back to first-world medicines if I had them handy.

The next morning all the women in the compound greeted me. It was nice to hear from both Mercy, my maid, and Ifeyinwa, that everyone liked me and thought I was very brave. I don't think I was at all like they had expected. I realised if I were to contribute in anyway as the other women did, I needed to find work of some kind.

# CHAPTER 18

# NEW FRIENDS

I was settling into life in Agbor at 48 Umudein Street, when one day Mercy escorted me to meet Francis Loveridge, who was head of history at the Local College of Further Education in Agbor. He happened to be our neighbour, who lived only five minutes away with his wife and two children. I had mentioned to Bunny earlier that week that I was missing stimulating conversation and intellect, due to cultural and language differences. So, when he arranged this meeting, I was desperately hoping that we'd get on. Life could be lonely at times in the village as the only white woman who did not speak Igbo.

Francis greeted us at the balcony of his home. He was a tall middle-aged man from Ghana, extremely well spoken and seemingly keen to meet me. He had been told I wanted to meet him by his secretary, who was a distant relative I heard.

Most meetings amongst the people in Africa are arranged like this, as there are no communal meeting places apart from the churches or places to shop. The room we walked into was half office and half lounge, and it was obvious he loved books, so at least we shared something in common. This first meeting turned out to be the start of a good friendship, and we talked nonstop for over an hour!

I told him I had to find a way to help out with the money situation, as Bunny just never seemed to earn enough to keep us, but that I also had to be at one with where I lived. So essentially, I had to become "an African," but I wasn't really sure where to start. Francis offered to go to the library and get me a book he thought would help, called *The Return of the Gods*, by

Ulli Beier, featuring the sacred art of Susanne Wenger, and we arranged to meet the next evening so I could see the book and borrow it. However, in my role as new wife, I had to accept that it would be difficult to be friends with a man and sit alone with him in Agbor or in any of the small villages local because of the gossip, so I'd have to arrange an escort for all my future meetings with Francis.

Francis turned out to be a source of great knowledge for me about his people, and his enthusiasm and information definitely inspired my writing. Francis suggested that I go to the library and research the history of the African tribal religion, and I visited the library often after that meeting. I discovered the following through reading the *Igbo History Hebrew Exiles or Eri*, by Omegala Aguleri:

Igbo religion begins with the belief and worship of Chukwu or Chiukwu Okike (the creator of all things). Ani the earth goddess is the most important deity in Igbo social life. Any great offence is against the earth, and any custom is covenant of the earth. *Odi-na-na*—that is what people do or what happens in the locality of the people's land.

On my next visit to Francis, I took Mercy with me. After we'd had an interesting chat and were on our way out, we saw his neighbour's rabbit, which was kept in a tiny wooden cage, with hardly any food. I just wanted to release that rabbit there and then, but I knew it would cause an uproar and those kinds of things were just not done. It was so hard, as all my views on animals and animal rights were rushing through my mind, but I was also aware that I had no right to impose my British values upon these people.

As Francis was saying goodbye, I couldn't stop thinking, Please God, don't let that rabbit be in that tiny cage next week when I come here. I don't want to keep seeing it suffer!

Mercy and I did the five-minute walk back through the streets, and she greeted everyone she knew en route. I felt I needed to write down my experiences and thoughts over the last few days, so when I reached our room in the compound, I brushed the red dust from my word processor, whilst Mercy found some candles as we were half expecting another power cut in the compound. She begged me to teach her to read that evening, so we sat with her favourite book from my collection *The House That Jack Built*; she read it aloud by candlelight as she sat next to me on my small wooden bench. I shared my newfound insights about African tribal religion that evening with Bunny when he returned from the shrine, and we chatted late into the night together. Life was good as a wife, I thought.

The days were passing peacefully, and domestically we seemed to have things organised. Whilst I typed and wrote this book most days, Mercy would always be near me, cleaning the windows with vinegar and newspapers or sweeping, as Bunny had said she needed to help me keep things clean. I wrote for a few hours each day and then started my washing by hand as there was no washing machine. Oney was a good cook and cooked daily for Bunny and me; plus, he boiled the rainwater on the little stove for my African shower daily. One of the main questions I got asked from friends at home was how I managed to do my laundry with no washing machine, but actually, it was easy to manage. The women of the shrine took my larger items as Bunny paid them a little money for this. They would wash everything with the local green soap, which smells really dull and very soapy. But everything seemed to come out very clean, and I would hang my clothes over the bushes or on the piece of string with a few pegs. However, I refused to allow my underwear to be washed by the women as I considered those items private, so I washed them by hand in a tin bucket. I must say I did notice my underwear was slowly getting bleached by the sun, but it was my new way of life. In fact, I often forgot about washing machines unless my friends mentioned it in their letters.

There was a thing about menstruation there in Bunny's lifestyle and his religious beliefs, as menstruation meant you were unclean. So, it was frowned upon for a woman at that time of month to be known to be sleeping with a chief priest and holy person. It was understood that the chief priest had to be clean in every way and not tarnished by an unclean woman. Definitely sex was not the thing to do one week per month. In fact, Bunny was not even supposed to be in our martial bed and be naked next to his wife I was informed. We did compromise eventually, and Bunny would lie next to me but would wear his long white shirt as protection.

Most days I chatted happily to Mercy in pidgin English, which scarily was starting to become second nature to me now. She was becoming a good friend, even though she was only twelve years of age. An uneducated dark black African, whose past story was a bit of a mystery. We knew that her mother couldn't afford to feed her as they were very poor, so she was offered as a maid to the family. Maybe that's why we got on so well, as I guess we both felt like outsiders. However, I still didn't feel comfortable giving Mercy too many domestic-type jobs, probably because we'd become friends, and also because I wasn't used to having a maid. So, we struck up a plan that she would wash the clothes and clean the red dust from the windows in the compound in exchange for me teaching her to read. So that was how it was between Mercy and me. I often wondered if she had been granted a good education and many privileges in life what she would become? But life was getting busy for me as Bunny's wife, and I was expected to attend his various religious or nonreligious events.

# CHAPTER 19

# ILLAH MEETING OF CHIEF PRIESTS

"What time is the vehicle coming, Bunny?"

"I've booked it for midday," he replied.

We were due to hold a meeting with all the chief priests at the king's house. I had typed out invitations on my word processor, and everyone had busily distributed them by hand.

I had decided to wear African clothes, and Mercy and I had made a special trip to buy a beautiful green-red-and-gold wrap of material from the market in Agbor. In complete contrast, Bunny was dressed British style, in jeans and a blue T-shirt! Sometimes I wondered if I got it all right—the dressing up or not business. I loved the women teaching me how to wrap the starched glazed cotton around my head; it looked so fanciful and covered my hair, which seemed to constantly need colouring as the constant shower and heat did nothing for it.

When I walked towards the car that day, it was full. There were four women worshippers, a chief priestess, Bunny, Mercy, and myself, pushing to find a space and opening a window so that we could breathe. A journey in one of those taxis was always an adventure to Illah along those crazy red dusty roads. In Britain, such a car wouldn't be allowed on the road, as it would never have passed its Ministry of Transport (MOT) test. I noticed its speedometer was broken. Goodness knows how fast the taxi driver was driving, and yet it seemed he never stopped talking. He seemed upset that we had refused to pay more than 2,000 naira for a return trip to Illah and back. The taxi was now full with eight of us, and of course all that weight was doing nothing for its suspension or his temper. But this seemed the normal behaviour that one negotiated the price, and the driver seemed to agree; then he would moan, and you always finished up giving him a free meal, or a big tip, or both.

I was wearing my full tribal wear as we stopped for petrol. Then Alice (the king's third wife) decided to buy bananas through the window of the back of the old Vauxhall saloon car. I thought of the British motorway stations where you'd pull up and walk into a spotless shop and buy from a range of goods on shop shelving with price tags and about how much more civilised and very different that all seemed from my current reality. Of course, we had a new visitor amongst us now. That was Ugegbe, a very important high priestess from Agbor. She was in her late forties—a tall, buxom lady with a very loud, bossy manner; she had a large shrine in the village of Agbor herself. Plus, she had family abroad about whom she loved to tell us. All locals, I noticed, who had sons or daughters abroad always boasted that their extended family had managed to get out to either Germany or Italy or America and had somehow become rich. But no-one ever told you what their actual jobs were. She was very proud, held her head high, and would often do divination when you least expected it or burst into song and ring a bell and pray. She was amazing!

Today, she was immaculately dressed as usual, with her hair braided into tiny plaits, and she'd even stuck a small red feather on her forehead, attached by the plaits. She looked very tribal as she sat haggling through the window to get a decent price for the carrots that a young street seller was trying to sell her. I could tell that he was annoying the priestess as he was invading her comfort zone by pushing the carrots right under her nose as she sat in the front of the car. The chief priestess was speaking loudly and firmly so that she got the best price possible. She said that she was sent money from her sons on a regular basis, so she could afford to be kind. I noticed she was always buying drinks and kola-nuts to impress us all.

As we travelled, I started singing the chorus of an African song, and the high priestess joined in leading the verses. The singing is a little like gospel singing, where the preacher sings the first line and the congregation repeats it. The mood was happy. I glanced at my watch. We were one and half hours late. The meeting was due to start at 1:00 p.m., but due to Bunny's rank, it was only right he would arrive late with his entourage of people.

The car pulled up next to the king's house. Fifteen or so people were seated on the large porch. The women were brightly dressed, and each sported large brightly waxed cloth tied around their heads (typical female Nigerian headdresses). That day I regretted not bringing my camera along.

The now-familiar drumming had begun. Two men dressed in bright yellow kaftans with Arabic embroidery sat beating hypnotic rhythms out. Oney had arrived earlier and was very excited to see us. He greeted us enthusiastically and quickly led the way into the main bedroom of the house, keen to show me where I would sleep that evening. The house resembled a very large bungalow with seven bedrooms with no stairs; it looked on to a large piece of flora and fauna. You could see the banana plants when you took an African shower. The front piece of land was where all the women and children prepared the food and cooked it over bamboo fires. The house did not have a fitted kitchen or running water. The eldest daughter would squat in the corridor near the side door, pounding yam with a large wooden stick in a large, old wooden container. I knew Bunny had no intention of staying overnight when we set out, but we never knew how long things would take once we began visiting people or holding meetings So, I thanked Oney for clearing a room for us.

I looked around for our luggage, and before I knew it, the bags had already been placed near the bed. I suspected one of the women had emptied the car boot on our behalf.

Everyone was busily greeting each other on the porch, so I made my way through the house to greet the king. He was seated on his four-poster bed. He was dressed in loose white robes; when he rose to greet me, his clear eyes sparkled as he looked up at his new Nigerian daughter-in-law with her newly braided hair. He was clearly very proud of Bunny's choice of bride (we had met only once before). I bowed to him, and we held hands as I shuffled up next to him on his bed. The king's head was shaven, and he was dressed in a long white cotton shirt. He looked bright and happy. I bent down to give him an affectionate kiss on the cheeks—a British greeting I felt.

"So many people in my house," he said.

"Yes, Bunny and I have summoned them for a meeting," I said.

"Good," he simply replied.

A bottle of Coca-Cola stood between his feet as he dangled his legs over the side of his four-poster bed. It seemed a strange sight, to see something so modern, branded, and international by the king. He'd witnessed great things in his lifetime, from colonialism to Nigerian rule, had married fifteen times, and had sired ten children. He had built over twelve shrines in Delta State and had launched Awucha (African tribal religion), but now, there he was sitting on the end of a bed, drinking Coca-Cola.

The king wanted to stay in his room and watch the dancing through the window. He was tired. He had greeted many visitors that day. I joined the dancers, much to their surprise, and they gave a loud cheer as I took my place amongst them in a tribal dance on the porch; many of the women shook my hand and thanked me for trying to be one of them. The women grabbed Bunny and forced him to dance with them, pinning money on our forehead as was the custom. The atmosphere was joyous.

Once the mood settled and everyone was seated, the speeches began. This was the standard method of communicating. We had no post, as such, so the only way you could get help or spread any news was with storytelling and speeches about our intentions.

I passed Bunny his speech notes so he could talk about our intended plans. There were other speakers too, but the funny thing about making a speech in an African village-type gathering is how when the person wishes to hold his audience, he will suddenly burst into song—then everyone else joins in. It's a marvellous attention grabber, but I can't see it working in the UK. It would be strange if UK business people tried it, though. It would be amusing to use this method in offices and boardrooms. I wonder what people would think if suddenly a good rowdy song was heard. They'd probably think the director had opened the drinks cabinet!

I glanced at Bunny's mother cuddling a shrine baby belonging to one of the women. She was so naturally maternal. She and I were so different. She had spent her life bringing up children. She had very little schooling, if any, and was completely illiterate. She had worked on the land, farming crops for the family, and had met Bunny's father. Then at the tender age of nineteen, she had started having his children. And, now that she no longer had any small babies, her main role was mothering and nursing the king, now that he was bedridden, and sometimes still helping on the family farm.

When it was her time to speak, she dropped her head, and I could see a bald patch where she had lost her hair through carrying very heavy firewood on her head each day. I couldn't understand what she was saying but guessed she was begging for money or assistance for her hard life. She would often do this. Bunny looked slightly embarrassed as this was not what he intended, and he must have felt he was losing his grip on the meeting, but he was too polite to ask his mother to be seated. She then proceeded to start recalling old stories. I noticed the meeting was degenerating into chit-chat and our major objectives were being lost. Fortunately, the high priestess, a close ally to Bunny, was next, and she held the audience's attention. She stood in the circle and waved her arms and commanded the audience with her husky Nina Simone-type voice. When her speech was relayed to me later, I found out she had pulled everything together for us and repeated all our requests. Good for her.

It was getting dark, and the taxi had arrived to take Bunny, myself, and our entourage back to Agbor. So, we hurriedly said our goodbyes. Only a few hours before, we had consulted the oracle, an ancient method of divination, and when the king read the oracle, he said we'd not given thanks to the shrine for all the good things that had happened, like us meeting, the wedding, feasting, and drinking. All these events had occurred without us thanking the shrine and pleasing the gods of Awucha. We needed to give thanks and say our prayers before we left.

Bunny led the way into the shrine outside the king's house. I helped the king walk as he struggled with his walking stick, and Bunny's mother followed. We entered the shrine after cleansing ourselves, which involved putting alligator pepper into our mouths (alligator pepper resembles black pepper, but it very hot), circling our heads with the pepper seeds twice, and then pulling our blouses or shirts forward to bow our head and spit inside our clothing to cleanse ourselves. Then sometimes spitting down our arms to cleanse those too.

I felt very embarrassed when the boiling hot pepper was burning the palate of my mouth and an uncomfortable sensation ensued.

"What do I do, eat it? Spit it out? It's very hot," I whispered to Bunny.

"Just spit it out if you prefer," he said.

Bunny's father's oracle consisted of four long pieces of string with large shells and pieces of ivory on them. The length of each string was about eighteen inches, and each shell had a different meaning and referred to a different god. Bunny's mother rang a large bell to awaken the gods, whilst Bunny offered a prayer in Igbo. Everyone seemed happier once the king's request for prayers had been granted. We returned to the king's bedroom, where the king seemed relieved to be able to climb on top of his four-poster bed to rest. Bunny and I had followed him there to be private, and the king allowed me to play with the oracle as he trusted me as the new wife in the house. I raised all the strings of shells as Bunny instructed and then drew them towards me on the floor area and then turned them over. We all stared at the floor in silence. I felt a strange sensation creep over the outline of my body; my aura was being checked by some outside force. I could feel it checking out my energy level. I had experienced these weird feelings many times before I drew a deep breath and thought only positive things.

"What do you see?" I asked Bunny.

"Lots," said Bunny in deep thought.

"Cast them again, they are still talking about what is going on in the house here," said Bunny.

I obeyed, and they were duly cast. When I glanced at the oracle, I got a vision of an office with long rows of people working in the UK.

"Oh, I feel I am visiting a new newspaper, with long rows of people typing. Three people are talking to me, but they cannot give me what I need. But they do actually lead to what I actually want.

I said. "That's interesting," said the king, "because you had never learned our ways, and you and I are new to each other, still this oracle, with all its gods and complexities, linked with you, and you got a message. Tell us what happens next?" "I see travel for myself and Bunny. I feel the spirits of past lives, of old tribal kings, here. But now it has all gone, and I see the floor here in your bedroom, and I hear the African voices fading."

I felt strange about that experience, but I knew the message was true and could happen to me. We then drank native gin to celebrate my initiation into the world of Awucha's tribal religion as wife and possible chief priestess-to-be to Bunny Ugochukwu Anikwe.

As the king stared directly at me, Bunny excused himself to organise the women and the cooking of our food. This intense staring was not new to me as I had experienced this before with the king; he could almost see through people with those piercing pale-bluey brown eyes, which I felt were unusual for an African. I was not going to let him see into my soul, so I attempted to hold the stare and smile, and it seemed to work. I had felt in the past meeting that the king was a strong chief priest in the region and well respected. But he always seemed to be checking me out. It was a little spooky, and I swear I could feel his powers right there and then in that room as we sat cross-legged, glancing at each other whilst he poured liquids onto cowrie shells. It was a weird yet comforting experience, a kind of meeting of souls and minds in one split second. There was a long silence before he spoke.

"I know," he said.

"Yes, I know too that you have been waiting to see me and that you knew that Bunny and I would meet, didn't you?" I said wisely.

"I knew a very long time ago of this meeting of my son and you. I saw it in my mind's eye," he replied. "Suzanne, you must write of our people and our line of Igbos and tell the world of us." he said as he leant forward. "I have kept all these rituals and my shrines, and Bunny needs to take all this in hand. But sometimes he is like a young man, and you must take care of him and record these many things as I am a king and chief priest here of my people."

I heard myself commit to it all! The diary was now officially going to be my first book. He passed me the runes, which were made of bones and cowrie shells. I cast them onto the floor of the shrine.

"What do you see for me?" said Bunny as he walked back into the room.

I said in a quiet voice, "I see the growth of your religion but not without a lot of effort and time passing. Then, I see travel for myself and then Bunny. I feel the spirits of past lives, of old kings here.

The king smiled and said, "You must come and see me again when you have become an African wife, and I will be here whilst you write, and we can drink coffee, maybe?" His eyes twinkled, and he smiled a smile of great acceptance.

Later Bunny and I left after thanking the king. Visiting Illah was to become one of my favourite places to visit with or without Bunny. I found the king so clever and wise. He told me that once in his life he had lost his sight for many years and that only through prayer and traditional herbs had he regained his sight again. He had been educated in English by the Christians who had arrived in Nigeria in the early twentieth century. He said that he had followed them around with their Bibles, and once he had even converted to Christianity. He had improved his English language skills by travelling with them and studying the Bible. But he changed to tribal religion later.

Just before we left he asked us to sit on the porch with him and watch the sunset. The king said he wanted to see photographs of my mother and father, then he stared at my father's very white hair and smiled.

"I knew my son Bunny had found you right from time," he said. (Translated—he knew that Bunny had found me as he has seen it as a vision "Now I know you are real and, I can rest," he said.

Bunny thought that his father was waiting for that very day when we had arrived to finally relieve himself from the power of the shrine, which Bunny and his followers said was keeping him alive. As it was now getting late we stayed the night and the next day we returned to our compound in Agbor for Bunny to begin his own chief priest's duties.

# CHAPTER 20

# SLAUGHTER DAY IN AGBOR

Within days of being back in Agbor, our lives went back to their normal routine. Bunny rose early and headed off to the shrine. I would sit and write on the porch. We were excited about our plan to organise a festival as we felt this was a good idea, although we had no idea how to fund it. We thought that perhaps it could take place there in the shrine as the shrine was in the grounds of the compound. We had sought permission from the church next door to go ahead. This was to get them to allow us to be very noisy.

I heard Ugegbe's, the high priestess's, husky voice greeting Bunny in the grounds jovially. She was altogether a real larger-than-life lady, who was worried as she had family troubles; a pending divorce was on the cards. In this part of Africa, divorce was looked down on as marriage was taken very seriously. She had come to talk it over with Bunny. And I had a morning planned of writing. The high priestess had apparently been looking after the shrine whilst Bunny had travelled. She was not too happy, it seemed. They talked for a long time whilst they drank native gin, rang the native bell, and said loud prayers. I hoped that it would help her.

At midday, I visited the shrine to see Bunny and found him sitting inside with a young man who was suffering with bad dreams and evil spirits. They sat talking in Igbo. Then the young fellow sped off on his motorcycle to the market. He had been sent on a mission. He later returned with a baby chick, a fully-grown chicken, and a fresh egg, plus bits of red cotton, black cotton, and white cotton. I watched as the chicken's egg was wrapped in the cotton threads, almost as we would dress an Easter egg up, whilst the young man, who was about thirty years old with shaven head, was repeating a chant over and over to ward off his evil. Then I saw my husband do something I'd never seen before, and it totally repulsed me. He lay the baby chick down, its yellow fluffy down spread across a small black cloth in the yard of the shrine. Then he quickly cut its head off. It lay motionless against the kola nuts—which had been blessed—next to it. They chatted together in Igbo; then the guy returned with the mother hen and placed his feet across her ankles, crouched down, twisted its neck full round, and cut its head off also. I was witnessing mass decapitation, or so it seemed. I looked away; my stomach turned. It was all so barbaric.

Bunny took the remains of the mother hen and rubbed it against the bark of the tree in the middle of the compound yard. Then the young man cut off its legs and feet. Bunny returned to do divination of the egg and chick and kola nuts. They wrapped the items of birth and death into two black cloth parcels. Bunny told him to bury the black cloth parcel containing the fresh egg in the local graveyard the other parcel was to be thrown on the express highway.

Even though I didn't want to think of the cruelty I'd seen early, I was curious and asked Bunny the meaning of it when I saw him later. Apparently, the egg in the graveyard was for protection from evil forces, and the chick on the expressway would protect him against accidents while travelling as the young man was a motorcycle driver on the busy expressway. I hoped that this would give him protection so the animals hadn't died in vain. Most of the slaughtering seemed to be of chickens or chicks or goats or rams, although occasionally, for a very big spell, they would kill a cow. I was struggling with my feelings concerning the slaughtering again. It was so different from my Christian beliefs and my English way of life. I wondered how I would ever come to terms with it.

Pius Obuseh…Water Diviner, Agbor
The next day an old man came knocking on the compound door very early in the morning, and Bunny rose early to let him in. They quietly passed through the compound to the shrine at the back and sat chatting in Igbo

about the art of divination. It seems the very old man, who was dressed in white, was a water diviner, who was used by the locals to help them find suitable water spots for their own wells. He drank native gin with Bunny, and they cast the cowrie shells and chatted gaily. When he passed my porch, where I was busy typing on the word processor, he waved his thin arm and bade me well. I wrote this poem as he walked off into the red dust of Agbor.

Pius Obuseh…Water Diviner, Agbor
*The herbal man*
*Of water spirits*
*He knew great things*
*Fluidity and movement*
*Water calling his way*
*A diviner of water gods*
*Bathing, searching for spirits,*
*Seeking water children*
*Magician and seer*
*Watery things summoned*
*Healing, dowsing, assisting*
*Poor and rich seeking him*
*Greater things than you or I*
*Pius Obuseh great waterman.*

# CHAPTER 21

# ILLNESS

I t's important, I hear, not to collapse into the highs and lows of one's emotions during bad health, but I was struggling not to feel low. I'd been ill again with cystitis, which had plagued me since being in Africa. Although, if I'm honest, I had suffered with this complaint infrequently since being in my twenties, the water in Africa wasn't helping, being unclean compared to British standards. I was living on antibiotics, which I wasn't happy about, due to the long-term effects. Worryingly, I was beginning to need higher doses or different variations of the tablets to keep this "burning water disease," as Bunny called it, at bay.

Yesterday my bladder had felt swollen, and I was running a temperature. Thoughts of home loomed large in my mind. The drug I usually took in England would often cure it, but I could not get it there. The only drugs I could get just seemed to mask the problem, not cure it. Also, all the tablets seemed to be weaker than the ones at home, and I was never sure if they were genuine. I seemed to be living on antibiotics, and I was not happy about that.

Today I felt weak, too weak to talk, so I was just silent, inclined to introspect. I felt as though someone had wrung out my kidneys. It seemed that illnesses were often the only thing that brought me to my senses.

Mercy saw a live scorpion in my room that day and said that someone had planted it there to kill me and that I should be careful. I didn't panic. I just splatted it with my flip-flop, and she ran out screaming that it was a curse and that someone wished me ill. I did not believe her for one moment, but it unsettled everyone in the compound.

What the hell am I doing here? I thought. Even a cold February in England must be better than this! I am living with no running water, no comfortable chairs, no carpets, no hot water (except when boiled over an open fire), no cooker, no decent food, no decent free doctors or medicine in sight, and no such thing as the National Health Service.

I felt sad about everything. Sad that I'd not seen the TV or heard my own tapes for over six months. Fed up of there being no landline in the compound, just one public phone at the post office where you had to queue for hours, and then the staff at the post office could hear you as they were in the same room. "Nothing is private" I heard myself say. Those people in that office also timed your call-in order to charge you. No postal system to your door, only a postal box that you have to pay for when you collect your mail, and sometimes the post is already opened by the time you get there. You may wonder why I felt negative. Well, the money Mom had sent me for my birthday present inside the card had been stolen. It was just a day when I had to get everything that I was fed up with in Africa about off my chest. I tried to look on the positive side most days, but this seemed like the last straw. It was absurd, as everything else was fine. I had a great family and a gorgeous, loving husband. I was cooked for and cared for, which is a lot more than most have.

I decided that the best thing would be to get another shot of penicillin into my thigh at the back of the local chemist shop, so I could stop moaning and do something positive, such as to get busy creating my latest sculpture with the local clay again.

I looked out of the window and remembered my past life in Wolverhampton, where I had attended an evening sculpture class for over four years and learned to sculpt statues in clay. Yes, I thought, I could teach the children here to really sculpt and maybe even sell some of my own work to help us out moneywise. Also, I was now keen to begin sculpting, perhaps even create a mask or two to hang in the shrine. This was my plan and gave me a purpose. I needed to get as busy as I could. Now tomorrow, I thought, I'll take a shower and get myself together; after all, the women here don't moan. I noticed they seemed so strong, and they never complained about their lives too much. I decided I needed to learn that when in Africa, learn to be an African!

# CHAPTER 22

# THE PHONE CALL AT PETER'S HOUSE

A few days later when I was feeling brighter, I decided to head out early evening to see some friends—Professor Loveridge, the history professor, who was my new family friend and Peter Nwakor, a local friend of the family. We sat on Peter's porch, drinking water and passing the evening. Peter was the chairman of the local government there in Agbor. He was well read and very well educated, with a small family. His wife was a kind lady and a devout Christian, who loved to chat to me about travel and education. She was the chairperson of the local Girls Brigade. The pair were great hosts, so I enjoyed spending time with them.

Peter's garden was a delight at night. His house was at the end of the road and faced a green bushy area with an amazing view. Fortunately for Peter, although the view looked fantastic, it was actually swampy ground, meaning no one could build a house there and spoil his view. Peter, Francis and I would discuss news and events, putting the whole world to rights, there on the porch. We noticed in the paper that Mike Tyson, the boxer, had bitten Evander Holyfield's ear and was to be suspended from boxing. So, we chatted about this and about Mother Teresa, who had died in Calcutta. Tony Blair was prime minister in the UK, and Lady Dianne was in the news, banning landmines. Our newspapers were a week old and very expensive to buy, but we tried to keep abreast of the times as best we could. Peter's wife was travelling to Australia with the Girls Brigade Association. We spent a long time discussing how long it would take for her to get there. She often spoke frankly to me; she often wondered why I continued to live in hardship in Agbor.

"Don't forget where you came from, Sue. Bunny's people eat meat that has been killed in ceremonies."

"Well, I was going to bring you some spare goat tomorrow that we will be slaughtering tonight," I said jokingly.

"No, sorry. We can't eat it, Sue, it's against our religion" she replied quite seriously.

I always felt Peter's wife meant well, but I wondered if she thought that either I should completely convert to African tribal religion or Christianity, or just head back home to England.

As the night wore on and we discussed England and my family being there, etc., I asked Peter whether I could use his landline phone to call home. I was conscious that I'd not spoken to my mom for a while, but I still felt a bit cheeky asking. He said I was more than welcome to, so I called Mom and asked her to call me back. She asked about my health as usual. She was delighted to hear that my cystitis and tummy bugs were over, but I didn't tell her about my lack of periods.

She gave me family news and said she loved me and missed me. My mom's calls were really important as we had no Internet facilities in the town then, and Mom's letters were only about two pages long. Sometimes it would be the only British voice I heard from week to week on that phone. Not one British person lived in Agbor or visited during my stay there so I often felt very alone.

Thankfully Helen and Marian, my dear friends, would send me nice letters, which actually were the nearest thing to girly conversation I could get.

# CHAPTER 23

# WITCHCRAFT IN AGBOR

Just as I thought I was used to Africa and its way, one Saturday in March opened my eyes again to the country's surprises, as I suddenly heard Black Moses, the Rasta, shouting loudly.

"Quick, look!". I was standing with Bunny on our porch, looking onto the streets where there was a crowd gathering, causing a rowdy commotion, as the dust gathered around their feet.

Through the dust I could see the crowds shaking their fists and shouting after a lady in our streets. They were all very angry, chanting after a lady in our street.

"They have come to lynch her or stone her, I think," said Black Moses.

"Whatever has she done?" I said.

"She killed her two sons," said Moses.

"How do you know? Where are the police anyway?" I shouted.

No-one replied on the porch; they just looked on in silence. Then Moses commented, "She admitted killing them. The second boy has just been brought back from the hospital without a mark on him." The daughter had locked the body in the room and run off with the key, leaving the mother behind, who was now being accused of witchcraft.

This was street justice that I was witnessing. The crowds were furious and wanted to kill her. The chanting got louder and louder, and the mob moved faster and faster down the street chasing the woman, saying she was a witch.

We heard later that she had been beaten up and someone had cracked her head with a cement block and that they wanted to lock her in the room with the decomposing body of her son. This was barbaric but it was street justice I was told. The police eventually came and took control of this crazy scene. The people that day obviously thought their actions were right.

I had read somewhere that it is impossible to be bewitched by someone or something if you do not believe in witchcraft, and I hoped that was true! We sat around the fire that evening, and Moses regaled us with all he knew about witches long into the night as he played his guitar and sang reggae songs.

Moses said, "Well, they often poison you slowly, very slowly, or just even point one finger at you, and this can make you very ill."

Bunny asked for the nonsense talk to stop and told Moses that he should get busy working on some jobs for him. Such as going to the market for items and composing a list of items needed for food for the compound for the next day. That always stopped the long stories, which were slightly exaggerated but nevertheless entertaining.

As with many things in Africa, I couldn't get the scene out of my mind—having never seen anything like that in England. I wondered if psychologically the mother was depressed and perhaps that because of the great poverty she was experiencing, she may have done this or if it was someone else? I will never know the real reason. All I knew was that there didn't appear to be any kind of mental institutions there or even counselling. People just called mentally ill people "insanes." They dealt with them by keeping them with their families or sometimes putting them in shackles at that time. Africans did not believe in sending people away from the tribe. They would always try helping each other, but if people committed a big crime like killing or making people sick, they had to suffer jungle justice.

"You see what a big job we have here, Sue," said Bunny as he took off his flip-flops to come to bed that night.

"Yes, it is very scary how they react sometimes. I am so glad the police arrived and dealt with it though," I said.

"Well, I will be meeting with the chiefs here tomorrow as we cannot have this unrest or bad behaviour. We will have a very early meeting to find out the truth tomorrow. Do not worry yourself," said Bunny as he kissed my cheek before falling asleep.

I could see how Bunny's travels were going to help him as a leader, as he'd seen enough of Western ways to know that this was not the modern way of dealing with such issues.

However, Bunny's kingship was to be in Illah, not in Agbor, so he really could not be too forceful in this issue. All he could as a chief priest was to insist that chiefs and elders did not behave like this in the future as it was barbaric.

I thought of the high priestesses that night and the power of the women around me. I sat and wrote this:

Female Shrine Power

*High Priestess, High Priestess*
*Such power you yield*
*In your African headdress*
*Men and woman bow to you*
*Children gaze at you*
*Seer of great things*
*With your herb medicines*
*Healing all from afar*
*Ritualistic in your methods*
*You scatter your white chalk*
*A dominating presence*
*You rule your Awucha jungle.*

That March, Esther arrived to live amongst us, under Bunny's care. Esther was a small light-skinned girl, eighteen years of age. She was pretty with short hair and large brown eyes. She was defined by her family and friends as an insane (which was the African term for a mentally ill person).

The pastor of the church next door had washed his hands of her. The family congregated in the shrine area to ask for Bunny to cure her. Although I couldn't understand the language, I found out much later that the family had already spent over 11,000 naira paying the pastor for treatment over a three-month period. The pastor, using God's powers and much prayer and laying on of hands, plus a strange ritual of an olive placed in a dish of olive oil, still hadn't cured her. I heard Esther's voice during her stay, singing hymns nonstop as she sat on the church wall behind our room. Always she was alone; the locals chose to ignore here as they realised they could not do anything for her. The neighbours fed her, and her mother collected her and paid the food bill. Bunny called her to the shrine to pray with her to the gods of the shrine to help, and also, she drank one of their medicines from the forest to keep her calm.

Esther had nowhere to go it seemed, and it made me think about mentally ill people there in Africa. Many do not get adequate help. There are no homes for the mentally insane. In the Delta region, many of the families have to cope with their mentally ill family members alone.

Whilst it's nice that the mentally ill people get to stay with their family, it's a huge drain on the family's resources and time, as the insanes often cannot work and are sometimes physically disabled too, especially girls. On this issue there's the problem that they're often sexually developed and so try to escape to get a boyfriend! We used to have to keep watch in the compound to make sure any mentally ill young women, did not escape to have sex, especially unprotected sex, as that was another problem for everyone. Unprotected sex could lead to more children, and our guest Esther could not cope with that herself. So, if she had become pregnant, it would have led to a whole new set of problems for the family.

It seemed that all Esther wanted to do was pray or sing all day. We had to encourage her to eat, but there was no way that she was going to mix with the community.

After three days her family came to collect her, and we guessed that they would do a tour of all the healers and churches to try to find a solution.

Seeking help in Nigeria can be a problem, as many poor people can't afford to pay a doctor for the tablets and treatment. In all my time there, I never saw a family-planning clinic for women in that area. Maybe there were some established later but definitely not in the 1990s. I often worried about this, but I was helpless to do anything with no money and no real voice there. We take so many things for granted in England, and until we travel more or even live amongst these tribes and really experience such things, we cannot begin to imagine the heartache of the mother of children like Esther and similar families, who may be dealing with sons and daughters who were mentally ill. I had studied counselling back home and wondered whether there was any way I could help, but on reflection, I decided the language barrier was just too much of a hindrance. Esther was not interested in communicating with anyone; she lived in her own little world full of Christian songs.

When I awoke the next morning, the family had already collected Esther. Bunny returned to our room, silent, as he was upset that he couldn't cure her as quickly as they needed.

"I cannot help her in time, Sue. The spirits need longer for her."

"Bunny, you did your best. Please don't worry. There will be many others we can help. I am sure." "I am on call night and day, and still it is not enough for them all." "Bunny, please rest. You cannot save the whole world."

"I can only receive messages from the gods and do my best, but sometimes it is not enough. I wish we had a bigger shrine and a hospital for them to rest, Sue. What we've got here in Agbor is not enough maybe one day I will get my chance here."

How could I even begin to explain to him how in England everything was so very different with trained staff, modern facilities, and even special hospitals for mentally ill people. Having all these things sometimes that is not enough to help all the people! He wouldn't believe it if he saw how some mentally ill people can live a relatively normal life on medication and special care. It would seem archaic for people in any first-world country to witness mentally ill people wearing shackles in their family home.

Later, Bunny lay on the bed, as the midday sun scorched the grass and everything in sight. I watched the children playing in the compound for a while, thinking how lucky they were to be healthy. Then I went to visit my clay masks to sculpt a little more.

I thought of my job back home and what a far cry from all the deadlines this was. I thought of my training in counselling and how that would come in useful in the future too but not unless I really got a grip of the Igbo language. As my husband slept, I stayed on the porch to protect him from the constant hassle he was getting from needy people.

When Bunny awoke, he switched put the BBC news on the radio, our only way of keeping in touch with the world. We relaxed as we heard what was happening outside our compound, as it helped to put our own problems into perspective.

Later that day, Simply Red played loud on the cassette deck, and Oney strummed his guitar as the sun beat lazily down on the porch. He would often be joined by a man named Friday, who was a local musician. He was a tall, lean man, who seemed quiet and studious. Often Ojo would play alongside Friday and Oney, and they would jam together and laugh and sing into the night. So, life was an easy pace for me, and I did my best to learn the language and to try not to embarrass Bunny with my bad Igbo skills or by being too English that I alienated myself. It was not easy to fit in sometimes, but everyone seemed to be kind. The evenings passed quickly. We had to amuse ourselves because we had no television, just a radio cassette player. When the mosquitoes began to bite, we would light the candles, and when the musicians had their break, Bunny would play Peter Tosh or Bob Marley, and we would dance or sing along. Then the tribal songs were sung on that porch.

Even though, as I said, we covered our bodies up from the mosquitoes, it was inevitable that sooner or later we would catch malaria. I had long since stopped taking my larium tablets. They were so expensive there. I was living on the breadline; money was so tight. As regards comfort our evenings consisted of sitting on the plastic mats put out to catch the cool breeze when the power was off in the compound. This was caused by electricity cuts from NEPA, the power provider.

Time was passing and nothing is more measured than by looking at the children around you, Mercy was now growing breasts. I noticed as she danced, and I started worrying about her playing in the puddles after the rainstorms with all the boys. I tried to stop her disappearing sometimes, but it was hard work. She wanted company. She was almost illiterate, and

I was persevering with reading lessons, but we were still on *The House that Jack Built* book. I worried about her education but decided we should soldier on and persevered with the same book until she had grasped the basics of reading. She was so full of life and very exuberant but always a pleasure to have around. She was now keen to help me to clean the house daily. Our curtains were held up with a piece of string and a couple of old nails, but Bunny and I didn't worry about those things.

In order to practise their music, Oho, a Rasta musician, came to share our house for weeks. He spent his daytime making badges in leather to sell on the streets. He would go out hawking during the daytime. It was strange because Ojo looked very similar to Bunny with his long dreadlocks, large mouth, white teeth, and long shiny ebony legs. The only difference was that he was a younger version of Bunny. When people commented about the similarity and asked if he was the younger brother, Bunny was annoyed. But Ojo only laughed at everyone's comments. Ojo was too busy making a living either making leather necklaces or working at his hawking to listen to the women's idle talk in the compound.

Black Moses, bunny & friends

Sylvester and Oney, Bunny's brothers

# CHAPTER 24

# BENIN ADVENTURE

With Bunny distracted working in the shrine during April, I finally found time to travel to Benin to visit the museum. Bunny was never happy about me catching the local bus as he felt some shame about this situation. Most of the white people who lived in Lagos worked for the embassy or the charities and so had their own Jeeps with private drivers. So, for the only white woman in the village to be poor and have no transport continued to be an embarrassment for Bunny as a prince of his people. Bunny also worried about me being robbed or kidnapped, as my English looks and white skin made me an obvious target. I never carried my passport or wore jewellery for that reason, but I did miss my loss of freedom and liberation, but I knew Bunny was really only trying to protect me.

I was walking towards the bus station and reflecting about being the wife of a chief priest. Bunny would expect me to be seen and not heard. I was never allowed to argue or show my displeasure overtly for any of the tribal customs. I would often close my eyes and look away at the tribal goat killings. If I really wanted to air my views to Bunny, it would have to be in the privacy of the bedroom, or we'd go for a walk. Also, the added problem was that the walls of our bedroom in Gabor were paper thin. As we lived communally, the musicians and customers slept near us, so if we raised our voices, everyone would hear us and know our business.

Although people in the compound were very kind towards me, I often worried that I was too liberated even sexually to fit in long term. I have to mention that even our love-making had to be done silently, which was quite different from Western ways.

Finally, my thoughts went back to my location. I had read that people in Benin had on average life expectancy of fifty-six years and only forty percent of people aged over fifteen were able to read and write. Benin often felt like a giant anthill with swarms of people continually moving; women were working in the streets, selling and bartering with each other or serving you in a restaurant. I knew I would be well fed in Benin. One of the main meals is fufu, a dough-like substance made from yam and corn grown locally. Locals dip this into their hot, spicy pepper soup. It is similar to stodgy mashed potato to look at but very tasty, cheap, and of course filling. Bunny and his family would eat this with their right hand and not bother to use forks—always a difficulty for me, as a left hander.

Benin is similar to Lagos, as it is hot—in fact, very hot. My dress was clinging to my body, and my hair seemed to be permanently stuck to my head—not a very glamorous look. February through to September and October were the hottest times of the year; then one would get the harmattan winds from the Sahara, followed of course by the rainy season, which was delightful for a British like me to acclimatise to. Only in November through to the end of January was it really cool and dry. But always it was dusty and well populated, with good food and crazy, insane traffic. I heard mostly Yoruba being spoken in the centre of Benin, but occasionally some born-again Christians speaking English would board the bus and manically try and preach above the noise of the gears crunching and the chatter of the passengers. They would wave their Bibles around, wearing dusty white robes, telling us we were all sinners who needed to be saved. We would all join in a Christian song, and it seemed fairly normal. Just something that is all part and parcel of a day out in Nigeria amongst the locals.

Benin had a liveliness that seemed to draw me. The biggest interest for me was the museum. I had heard of the sculptures and artefacts there, and I'd been really looking forward to getting out and spending the day mulling over the treasures.

I disembarked from the hot, sweaty yellow bus, packed with the usual traders and families going about their business, where I had been squashed next to a window, sharing a seat with a woman with a child on her back. She had a live chicken in a small cage under her seat beneath her legs. I spent the journey thinking about the life of this poor woman and how hard it must be for her. She seemed so young and wore no wedding ring. She spoke very little but slept a lot during the one-and-half-hour journey. Occasionally her head would slump forward, and the sweat would trickle down her neck onto the simple white blouse, which had clearly been hand sewn and repaired on numerous occasions. She had the remains of braids in her hair. Most of the women, no matter how poor, would find a way to put braids in their hair. Her young baby was very small and strapped to her back. It was so beautiful and well behaved. I wondered how they lived. What conditions did they sleep in? I longed to talk with her. But I had heard her speaking another tribal language that I was not familiar with. It was not Hausa. I wondered if maybe she was from Senegal or Ghana, as I had never heard that language before, and I was starting to get used to the different dialects.

After the long journey on the hot, sticky, overcrowded bus, my bladder was bursting, and I hoped my cystitis would hold out until I could get to a pharmacy for tablets. As we entered Benin, young beggars ran up to the bus, selling fresh water. I was beginning to doubt the authenticity of the Nigerian bottled water in our village and wasn't sure about these either, but my body was craving fluids. So, I put my fussiness aside and purchased two for my museum trip.

The thing I was most excited to see on this trip was the bronze head of Idia, the mother of Esigie, the Oba of Benin during their reign in Benin. This bronze human-sized head was originally used to decorate the queen's own memorial altar inside the Benin Palace. According to its history as stated, the cast brass head relates to the sixteenth century. Queen Idia, the mother of Esigie the Oba of Benin ruled from 1504 to 1550. Its style depicted the wealth and power of this woman, and it was believed to have had iron pupils in the past. It had been in my mind since I attended sculpture evening classes in Wolverhampton in the Midlands. I had also tried to sculpt one, so I was looking forward to seeing it in real life.

The sweat trickled down my back as I made my way across Benin in the busy traffic towards the museum. I wondered where everyone else was, as there just seemed to be me and a couple of other visitors walking around. I had seen many voodoo-type artefacts in the chief priest's shrines and felt silly always asking Bunny and his family what they all meant, so it would be nice to find out more about these things in a museum.

When I had arrived at the museum, a middle-aged bald man was inside the museum, sitting on a chair, looking bored and sleepy. I guessed he had shaved his head because of the heat. He greeted me in pidgin English and told me not to take photographs. I sat in a corner in the museum and drew pictures of the sculpture of Idia and tried to work out how I could make another attempt at sculpting my own version of this back in Agbor.

I thought of Oxford in England, especially the Pitt Rivers museum there, which has the largest selection of African artefacts in the world. I wondered how the intrepid explorers had captured these scary voodoo trinkets without being cursed. I wondered if being kept in their display glass cases could control the juju's power.

I stayed in Benin long enough to try the hot pepper soup and then decided to catch the yellow bus home before the midday heat became too much for me.

On the bus home, the travellers and I had the usual preachers boarding the bus intermittently along the journey, but I did manage to sleep a little, holding onto my bag with my money in (always a good idea when travelling alone in Nigeria). Bunny was pleased to see me when I arrived home and was busy ordering yams from our bedroom and getting Mercy and Ifeyinwa to cook them with chicken for our evening meal.

I was motivated to try and sculpt more and encourage the local children to come along to the free workshops I'd started running at the compound. I had discovered I could get clay from the river bed and mix it with chalk to the right consistency in order to sculpt. I did not have a kiln, so I had to rely on the heat during the day to bake my work. The thought of doing a solid head of the size of the Idia enthused me. I had only made flat masks for the shrines and for a couple of private customers at that time. It was really a chance for me to work with the children again near the shrine. The children recently had come and made little animals and dried them on the walls of the shrine. Sometimes we would have a little disaster when they crumbled and baked and broke in the heat. I would have to make a similar one and put it back on the wall and then give it that child when it arrived. The children would run home, joyfully holding their animals and no doubt one or two would sit on a wooden shelf next to the rice. As regards the inside of the homes in Abgor, I had not seen many windowsills in the small hut-type homes. Every inch was used to store food and clothing and kerosene for the fires or white candles for night light. Instead of wardrobes, most poor families just had a piece of string from one side of their little room to the other, and the mother would drop the clothes over the line above their beds on the floor.

I was inspired after my journey out and couldn't wait to get to my word processor to write about the Idia bronze head. I'd also got one sculpture that I had been working on—of a mask, which I had made with the local clay. I sprayed it with the local gold spray called Mercedes paint and placed a couple of screws in the back. Then all I had to do was thread some string through the hooks, and hey presto, it could be hung in a house or a shrine. I also had the option of selling it locally. This was an exciting prospect and gave me a purpose.

The next week I decided to take another trip to Benin and try for some work as the masks were taking a long time to sell. I was to hear some harsh words and another woman's point of view about my choice of husband and lifestyle.

Today was special, "Yes, I've seen your CV and references," said Kate, the general manager of the newspaper in Benin City. I sat in front of her, discussing the possibility of me lecturing in media sales for them—another idea to make a living. We now needed the money badly. I had received a very positive response from department heads beneath her when I had written to the paper the week before. Things looked good. Opposite me sat a large television screen and radio to keep her abreast of the times. A long table stretched in front of me; photographs in large picture frames

were placed high along the edge of the wooden panelling. Africans decorate their homes differently from British people. When it comes to hanging pictures, they tend to place them too high, where they just gather dust.
Many of the photographs in people's homes are very old and discoloured.
They also place large calendars in their homes, the kind we hang in facto-
ries or offices. "Tell me of your husband," she retorted.

"Oh, he's fine, seeing people in the shrine today," I replied.

"I hear he is to be the tribal king in Illah, as he is the first son."

"Yes," I replied.

"Are you going to have a family?"

"Well, if it's God's will, then yes, if not, no." This was far too vague
for her enquiry. But how was I to know if I could conceive at my age? I
had suffered with endometriosis since I was twenty-three years of age, so
I knew it was difficult for me to not only fall pregnant but also be able to
carry a child for the full duration of the pregnancy. I was not about to try
and explain that to a stranger who was interviewing me. I could tell that
sometimes Africans don't appreciate vagueness, particularly concerning a
direct question on childbirth. It is fundamental to them, a woman's role.
Women's Lib still had a long way to go in parts of Africa. Female circum-
cision was still practised. Women were starting to rebel as many women
would suffer urinal infections, which repelled their husbands, plus many
died through blood loss and so on. A woman could have ten children, and
no-one blinked an eye. Bunny's mother, for example. Not many bothered
with formal contraception in my village as they did not have a women's
clinic near they really struggled with this.

"Having a baby is something you have to want. You can't just say you
don't know," she said.

"We'll see," I reiterated.

"You know these kings take a second wife, don't you?"

"Yes, but Bunny's not interested in all that."

"Oh, you would be surprised. They always go back to their tradition."

These kinds of comments I'd heard before, even if I tried to explain
things away about Bunny and I meeting whilst he was travelling. He had

been away three years and now held a very Westernised view of marriage. I knew he had no intentions of taking a second wife. It seemed the women were often trying to warn me, protect me even if you like. But you know love is blind, and who knows their husband better, a stranger or his wife?

"You would need to take a couple of mates if he had a second wife."

Mates? Mates? What did she mean by that? Perhaps they were to be lovers. Hadn't I left all that behind? Didn't they believe in the constitution of marriage? Didn't Africans have a much lower divorce rate than people in England? Weren't you supposed to meet your prince and live happily ever after? Or was I living in cuckoo land? What if I couldn't conceive would he find another woman?

I managed to bring the conversation back to business, and we talked about advertising and editorial and general problems in the marketplace that all newspapers suffered worldwide. The gap closed between us, and we began to gain rapport. Kate was not in a position to book me. She had severe restrictions on her budget. They had now gone private and no longer were a government newspaper, so I knew training was not high on her priority list at the moment. We managed to leave the door open for her to reconsider possibly September time. She discussed traditions with me a little more and enquired if I would be attending the wedding of the king's son in Benin Palace. As the girl chosen would be future queen when the king died, I agreed out of politeness to attend in April but I wasn't sure if I could afford. She said there would be crowds there. I said she may not spot me as I would be in African attire. She laughed out loud.

"Of course, I will. You might change your dress, but you can't really change the colour of your skin, can you?" I laughed, but deep down I felt that it was a racist comment and maybe she had not taken me seriously in a business sense. We shook hands, and I departed. I left disappointed. They needed my help but could not afford me.

The midday sun was blazing down on my body as I left, dressed in my pink business jacket and brown skirt. My mind was confused. Why didn't she think I would be content in my marriage? Were our cultural differences so great? Mixed marriages in 1997 in Nigeria seemed rare, or so it seemed. Could Bunny and I not find common ground and build a successful marriage? She didn't seem to think so, but she didn't even know me, and it was not her business after all to ask such private questions at an interview for a freelance trainer.

I picked my way across the city and stepped into the taxi to Agbor. It was full of people who sat in silence, listening to the rain as it began to beat down on our old, worn out heap of a taxi. The driver was preoccupied with his windscreen wipers, which occasionally worked. They had obviously seen better days; the rubbers screeched across the glass, and we had to keep stopping for him to wipe the windows. Still he drove far too fast, but no-one commented. The real crunch came when I said, "This is very dangerous." A man next to me clutching a Bible asked the driver to stop, and he stepped out, saying he valued his life. We all watched in silence as he stood on the roadside dressed only in white shirt and black trousers, sticking his thumb out for a lift. I had hesitated as I had stepped aside to let him out. I hesitated, should I do the same? No, Sue, I thought, you don't know the way home, and you are a foreigner here alone, and besides that, you could be kidnapped or raped. So, I crept back into the vehicle and said a small prayer under my breath for this to please not be my day for seeing my next life.

My thoughts went over that idea, next life. I had been brought up in a house where my mother was a Roman Catholic, my father aa atheist, and my sister and I had always been sent to the Methodist Church (John Wesley, the founder). So, what did I believe now? Well, after studying psychology and different religions for twenty years and travelling and living amongst a variety of religious denominations for the last nine months, I had become very broad minded. But always I had believed that I was a temporary visitor on this spaceship called earth. I had read that morning that there are two factors that determine which body we shall obtain in the next birth. The first is our karma, the reactions to our good and bad activities that were performed in this life and in previous lives; the second is our desire to enjoy particular sense objects (materialism). This is the belief held by Awucha members—almost a spiritualistic outlook. They believe in old souls and reincarnation, so Bunny and I always believed that. My mind flashed back to one of our earlier conversations on this matter in the Gambia. I remembered the wind blowing through our hair as we chatted about life and death.

"Of course, this is just a shell we are in at present," I said.

"I know it's not the end when you die here," Bunny said.

"Well, you just keep reincarnating, you know," I said. "Tell me, do you believe that we come back as the same as we left, like male then male or female then female, or maybe as an animal?"

"Oh no, we don't believe you come back as an animal. We still believe you come back as a human being," Bunny replied.

"I once read that the soul is unbreakable, unchangeable, insoluble, everlasting, immovable. I truly believe that, don't you?"

"Yes," Bunny replied.

"I wonder where I'll be buried, or which part of the world I'll finish up in?" I said.

"Well, you'll be buried in Africa under our house as a tribal king's wife should be."

"What! Under your house? Where? In the lounge?" I was making fun, but Bunny was deadly serious.

"It is the custom to bury your dearly beloved in the lounge," he said.

"So, you then remarry and make love in the lounge on top of me," I said in jest. We both laughed out loud as I agreed to come back and haunt him if he should do such a thing. Sometimes you have to see the humour about life and death.

"Agbor," the driver said.

I disembarked into the rainstorm, glad of a nearby motorcycle taxi service to get me home. It's very easy to get on a motorcycle in Agbor. You just flag down one of the drivers, and for a few naira's, you are soon back home. Of course, there was no crash helmet or special clothing, so you took your risks.

When I arrived back in the compound, I could smell more hot pepper soup cooking, and I soon settled down to eat and share my story of the most judgemental interview ever.

But I did wonder if I would ever be accepted by the business community there as long as I continued to hold my westernised views and stay married to a Rasta man. There were a lot of class barriers there amongst the people. Even the prejudice against Rasta's noticeable. I was not familiar with such ways, but I knew I would keep on trying in my life to dispel them regardless.

*www.premiumtimesnj.com.*

# CHAPTER 25

# RAIN DANCING IN M'BIRI

Our friend the king of M'biri shook hands with me, keen to see me again since our last visit. I had met him briefly a few weeks earlier when Bunny took me to see the town of M'biri. The king and I walked into a small café in Umunede, as he said he wanted to show me off and also, he said, for me to taste the native food. A strange sight was to greet us. Nine chiefs were seated at small wooden tables eating grasscutter meat. This grasscutter I learned, is a delicacy in Nigeria. It's a small hog-type creature that is poached daily by the villagers and sold for about 400 naira to eat with garri (a popular West African food, made from cassava root and dried and ground into a flour) and accompanied with melon.

The chiefs were all dressed in their finery (brightly coloured Muslim-style kaftans and loose trousers, plus red-coloured fez, Egyptian-styled hats.) The king knew them all and chatted to them as he pulled up an old wooden chair for me to sit opposite them. I felt self-conscious. I was not just the only white in the village but also the only female in the café. The king proceeded to buy bananas and mineral water for me to drink as I tried to eat the meat which tasted like tough lamb to me. He was so kind. He had invited us to the yam festival there in M'biri. He explained he was an old friend of Bunny's and knew Bunny's mother as she was from M'biri. He had a palace and many lands. Plus, he had invited Bunny and me to stay in the palace for M'biri festival that very afternoon.

The M'biri festival marks the beginning of the agricultural year and is a great day of festivity and dancing. It's as important to the farming community there as Christmas day is to us in England. The belief is that they can only hold the event if everything has gone well with all the crops and they have experienced a good year, although I hadn't heard of them not holding the festival before. Our first visitor in festival-fancy-dress arrived. It was a chief priestess, the chief of all the African traditional herbalists. She was dressed in a fancy-dress costume of cement sacks, and up the front of her sacking dress, she had pushed a large pillow to give her the appearance of being pregnant. On her ankles, she wore many bells and bangles that rang as she danced. In her hair were beads and buttons, and an old cassette tape was sewn into it too. She carried an old tribal fan that looked like something from an old Victorian film set. She began to dance, and people pinned money on her, as is the custom. Bunny and I went around the town visiting people. Many lived in small mud hut-type buildings of red stone or one-story cement-built houses with iron gates around them and wooden shutters for windows. Each house seemed to be full of lots of children. The custom would be that we would enter the house where Bunny invariably knew the occupants; then he would introduce me, we would sit in their lounge or in their yard where they cooked garri, and we would be offered kola nuts. Then, after Bunny had blessed the kola nuts by touching them with his hand and said a prayer as chief priest, we would eat them. As they were very bitter, I would just take a bite surreptitiously throw the rest away.

Then the men would drink illicit gin or beer, and I would be offered a soft drink like cola or Cresta Bitter Lemon. Then, after chatting for half an hour or so, we would move on. The lady in the cement sack dress seemed to be following us; she would begin dancing wherever we went whilst still collecting more money, which was now being pinned to her dress. Next, we made a visit to Bunny's mother's old house. The women were so excited to see Bunny with his new white wife. I was hugged and called "my wife, my wife" (a term of endearment) before being shown around the yard where the women sat cross-legged frying the garri. Smoke filled the air from the terracotta-style pots that were cooking the bright-yellow garri. The pungent heavily scented air could be smelt for miles. This garri would be sold at the marketplace as a source of money for the families.

An earlier conversation about death that Bunny and I had had kept coming back to me; the acute differences regarding our culture re-emerged as I was shown Bunny's grandfather's grave there—just buried in the garden with no headstone, just a tree stump.

This seemed so different from the British solemn event where we would wear black and be respectful and bury our loved ones in a graveyard. People stood on the grave talking, not like in England where you would never dream of standing on a grave, chatting and passing the time of day. I started to think about when Bunny would visit England, hopefully. I had heard that many Nigerians travelled to England and rarely did they come back, as once they visited, they seemed to be smitten with the UK. Often young men would find work there and send money home to their families. I wondered about Bunny; could he ever leave all his tradition and family roots behind? But, if we chose to stay in Nigeria, could I leave my roots and family behind? I felt really sad about the decision we might both have to make, and my mother's face as we said goodbye went visually through my mind. I remember her saying, "You won't come back. I know," and I felt her whole body shaking. The tears filled my eyes.

"I'll be back, Mom," I sobbed. My father stood behind her at a distance. He was never very demonstrative with my sister and me, but I knew he too was hurting. I loved them both dearly, but I knew it was time to wrench myself away and begin my new life in Africa.

I brought my thoughts back to my current reality. I realised I often found that my thoughts wandered back to my life in the UK when everyone around me spoke in several different African languages at these events. I guess it was my way of coping, as it was when I was alienated in large crowds by the language barrier that I'd feel my most homesick. Funny how you can still feel lonely even when you're surrounded by loads of people, just because you can't understand the conversations and join in.

A bottle of Coca-Cola was thrust into my hand by Bunny. "Come, we are going on Black Moses's old motorcycle to visit a chief before we go to the festival. He says we can borrow it," he said. "Drink up. Let's be off."

I gulped down the coke and pushed my mind forward away from homesickness. I glanced at my watch. At 2:45 p.m. the heat was still rising, and the whole village was alive, anticipating the afternoon's event. I need to mention the state of the dusty red roads and the fact that there were no crash helmets or motorcycle gear ever offered to anyone; you just took your chances. But many people used motorbikes and scooters, as it was a cheap method of transport, and it kept you cool as the wind would blow through your hair as you steered your way through the crowds and the long dusty roads, past the many farms and mangrove swamps.

It is custom that it should rain. They pray for it. I was wondering if this would happen. Bunny pointed to a piece of land near his mother's house as the bike pulled away. "That's mine if I want it. I could build on it. What do you think?" I was being shown a small piece of land full of banana plants that looked derelict.

Bunny was just full of surprises. You never knew exactly which pieces of land he owned and where. We visited his friend, and whilst his friend, a fellow chief, repaired the brakes and serviced the bike we had hired, we sat and drank yet more soft drinks. After half an hour or so, we made our way to the festivities by bike and were offered lots of food and palm wine. The king insisted on he and I having a photograph taken on his throne; plus, he wanted me to meet his two wives and see his many children.

So altogether, the night and day was a great success for the king's festival. I began to wonder if Bunny would want more wives and lots of children, and when I asked him in our bedroom that night he said, "I am more Westernised than that now, Sue. I have seen all the wives and children my father had, and I do not want all those people to care for. So, do not worry yourself."

"But, Bunny, it's your custom here, and they do this in Gambia because I met Mr. Sonko there, and he had three wives, and no-one bats an eye."

"Well, I am an intelligent man and have travelled many places, and I know better. So please do not concern yourself with all this. Maybe one day we will have a child of our own. If not, you can take one of my father's children, and that will be it."

We kissed goodnight passionately, and I felt the pain in my heart of no children—something I had felt for many years. He stroked my hair, and I drifted off to sleep in the African heat, whilst the drums continued into the night and the faint sounds of tribal singing was heard.

Soon we were to travel back to Agbor so that Bunny could resume his chief priest activities and run the shrine.

King of M'biri

The King of M'biri and I

# CHAPTER 26

# THE EYE INFECTION

We often visited Claira's shrine, which was situated at the back of her house in the garden in Asaba. She was a portly woman, who was very popular as a chief priestess herself and a very good healer it was said. It was less than one hour from us in Agbor and was a thriving town. Since becoming the administrative capital of Delta State, Asaba, it had an estimated half a million-people living there. The population of predominantly non-indigenous people in the city included Urhobos, Isokos, Ijaws, Ukwuanis, Hausas, Itsekiris, and Yoruba's, so I had no idea what anyone was shouting in that marketplace. It was heaving with market traders and shoppers that day, as we had fought our way through the markets and side streets that reached Claira's shop. Old men also seemed to be making a living from pushing metal wheelbarrows through the streets with people's luggage piled high as the owners chased behind, keeping a watchful eye on their belongings. It was an ingenious way of making a living, I thought. You paid up front and then ran behind, not daring to take your eye off your little man with his head down, pushing ahead through the throngs of people, goats, etc. Oney carried our bags and shouted to me as we weaved our way through this madness. Bunny was back at the shrine in Agbor dealing with visitors and would join us the next day.

It was always a pleasure to meet Claira, who was very popular and had quite a large following of Awucha members, who would all meet us there during the afternoons and evenings. As she owned a fruit and vegetable store the front of the house was always busy. Late afternoon the women would get ready in the back of Claira's house and put on their white cloths and tie white wrappers around their waists in front of the large mirror there. They would also put on a little make-up and put on flat shoes and any bangles or orange coral beads to celebrate in the African shrine. There would be chickens and goats and often baby chicks in that yard, which sat unaware that they were being purchased and fed, ready for their sacrifice. Oney would often be seen tightening his drum with fresh goat skin to play that evening, and I would be in Claira's room, enjoying the cool air, as the fan droned above my head. I would feel safe and enjoyed the quiet; it gave me chance to think as I continued to write this book in pencil in my large exercise book. I could not carry the word processor through all that bedlam, so I always wrote by hand and then typed everything up when I got back to Agbor. All day people would visit the shop and drink soft drinks and greet us all.

But we were all waiting for the evening when we would begin singing, chanting, and dancing. A bit like whirling dervishes, we danced around the shrine in an anticlockwise direction; each hoped to either reach a trance-type state and prophesy or just forget all their worries for the night and of course be fed with succulent goat's meat and rice. As I did not understand the Igbo being spoken, I would often have to guess by the mannerisms of the Awucha worshippers what they were discussing. Oney would sit near me and translate sometimes when he was not busy sorting out the goats or chickens. I would dance for a few hours and then retreat to my room in order that I could escape from seeing the animals being killed. That night there seemed to be a very big festival that they all had come for. But the rain beat down on us, and we had to stand under the tarpaulin that Claira had set up near the shrine. We held candles and sat on old wooden benches huddled together and waited for the never-ending rainstorm to pass. I got bored after several hours and retreated to the main house to rest. I went to bed early as there was no Bunny there and Oney had grown tired of translating and needed to play the drums for their entertainment that evening. I was exhausted by our journey and went to bed early that night. I lay resting, listening to the singing of the tribal songs being led by Oney, as they all repeated his lead in each song and laughed and joked whilst waiting for the never-ending rain to stop.

"Ouch!" A sharp pain shot through my left eye. I quickly removed my disposable contact lens. Something had infected my eye badly. It was as though a sharp knife was going straight through my left eye. I scrambled along the corridor in the dark of Claira's deep freeze, looking for my sterilised water, quickly making an eye bath as my eye was now on fire. I started to panic. I'd seen many people in Africa with eye infections that left them blinded. I was terrified as my vision blurred and my eyelid kept getting glued up. I wondered if it was conjunctivitis; I grabbed a mirror from my handbag and with a lantern gazed at my eye. I was horrified with what I saw. My eye was bright red; the lid was swollen, and I looked like I'd seen a few rounds in a boxing ring! I had plans to look stunning when Bunny arrived to join us all on Saturday. Now I wondered about all that. He had also been called to another shrine in the town on business so he would be arriving soon. I definitely had not planned to look like an ogre. I spent the next two days indoors, unable to stand the bright African sunlight. Claira nursed me and helped me with eye drops and paracetamol (the answer to almost everything in Africa), whilst I just stayed in bed. I prayed for my full eyesight to be restored. Always when I was sick, I would question what I was doing in Africa, subjecting myself to illness after illness. I wanted to be at home, sitting in front of a qualified optician to get some professional advice. I wondered how I was going to handle my role as his wife and what about the business side of things like all the promotion works for Bunny's religion and music when I was so ill. Or even worse, if I couldn't see for a while. Now that Bunny and I had decided to promote his shrine and perhaps even a festival if we could drum up enough interest. Soon, the worrying abated as I fell into a painful sleep alone in my room. It seemed everyone had gone home and Claira had retired for the evening. So, she had gone to her room to let me sleep in peace after nursing me.

I could hear the goats moving around the hall area as they had come into the house to shelter from the rain and sleep. Then suddenly, I felt something crawling on top of my sheet towards my head. It felt quite heavy and stank. I realised it was a large rat who was investigating who was in his room. I was terrified. I got all my strength together and shook the sheet.

Then, as I jumped up, the large rat shot under the hole in the floorboards. I was shocked. I had never encountered a rat before. I went out into Claira's lounge to see Oney lying on the floor.

He sat up and said, "What is wrong? You look ill. Are you OK?"

"Oney, a big rat has just run over me as I slept in there."

He looked surprised and laughed. "Well, you are bigger than him. Did you kill him, or send him away?"

"I shooed him off."

"You will be fine. Just forget it and sleep. We have a big day tomorrow."

I returned to the room and lay for what seemed hours, thinking about it all, before fatigue took over and I slept. I thought, this is a first, sleeping with goats and a rat in the middle of Asaba. I thought of Claira's kindness and how she had nursed me during the day there and thought I should not make a big thing of the rat as she might be offended. I had experienced a rat before in Agbor who had died inside the wardrobe and that smelt disgusting.

The next day Bunny arrived, and I told him the story as he gazed at my swollen eye. He just laughed at my innocence about the rat. That night, whilst I rested on the bed, he changed into his white robe and went out into the yard to begin the divination and to continue the meeting of the Awucha members as the night before the rain had stopped the event.

They danced well into the night and held discussions on raising funds towards their tribal religion. They also greeted new members and discussed rituals and medicines together in Igbo.

We made our way home to Agbor on Sunday, after Claira had fed us hot pepper soup and fufu. I now looked respectable as my eye had cleared of the infection. But the illnesses were to haunt me again, I'm afraid to say.

When I was back in Agbor, I took ill again with weakness and dysentery. Bunny sent me to the medical centre and asked for some blood tests to be done; again, they diagnosed me with cystitis. Was this illness never to leave me? I felt exhausted. From the neck down, I was numb as the pharmacist had injected me in the thigh with 750 milligrams of Zinecef

My hair was still damp from the rainstorm I had got caught in. The lantern still burned in our room. Lying motionless, I checked my watch;

it said 11:00 p.m., and I could see the smoke emerging from the mosquito coil. I was alone. I had slept five hours with the effect of the drugs, but now I was hungry and disorientated. I forced myself to move and made my way into the kitchen on the porch to check what food remained. There was tomato and fish sauce to be reheated with white boiled rice. I warmed it through and ate by candlelight, remembering how candlelight always made one's meal look more appetizing.

In England we always used candles to create atmosphere for romance plus I'd used them to decorate my table when I'd cooked meals for friends, but in Africa candles were a necessity due to the constant power cuts. The power company was called NEPA in Nigeria. The locals joked and said that it stood for Never Ever Power in Africa.

I began to wonder where Bunny was. It was now 1:00 a.m., I made my way in the dark towards the shrine. As I neared it, I began to feel afraid. I put my right hand over my heart. It was pounding like crazy. What was I sensing? Evil spirits? I reached the shrine, but no lights were on, just a little light from the stars that illuminated the courtyard. The only things in the shrine that had any colour were the one dead yellow bird hanging upside down and a few little baby chicks hung by their feet tied to the string. Just evidence of ritual killing gifts for their gods. A few snail shells hung upside down next to the yellow bird. (Baby chicks are hung to represent life and good luck.) I thought of the long, lingering death of these poor little creatures. I wondered how long it took the snail there to die upside down like that in his big shell. I felt as a person I was on the edge of becoming encompassed by this religion with all its barbarism and rawness. I couldn't see Bunny anywhere, so I decided to make my way back to our house. Then I saw him, flashing his torch, looking for me.

"Where have you been?" he said aggressively.

"Where have you been?" I replied angrily.

"Why are you asking where I've been?" he said.

"Because it's one in the morning, and any wife is entitled to ask where her husband is, isn't she?" I shouted.

"I was here," he replied. I was not sure of Bunny at that very moment.

"Bunny, you weren't here. That's why I went to the shrine. I haven't seen you since I took ill at 6:00 p.m.," I retorted.

He put his arm around me and said that he had left me to rest and he had been praying alone behind the shrine for answers to my constant weakness there in Africa. We chatted until late into the night before retiring to bed to cuddle and make up.

But to be honest, I was never quite sure what he had been saying to the gods, as the language was always a barrier to my full understanding of the religion. Was it all in my head? But I had to trust my new husband if I was to remain sane there. I could not be watching him night and day. Other wives had told me that they often had to turn a blind eye and accept that their husband may take another wife but if I had a child, that would give me security. I didn't agree with that logic, but I had chosen to live there, and I needed to get well and be strong in both mind and body too. So, I decided to forget it all and think of my future happiness there.

Thinking back on that incident, of course I was annoyed at him for not checking how I was. Bunny was not the most compassionate whenever I took ill. The shrine was taking over our life, and I needed Bunny with me. But I realised that many people in the surrounding villages came to the shrine because it was an integral part of their lives and their belief system. The shrine was the answer to everything, from illness, bad luck, unhappy marriages, stillbirths, barren woman wanting children, and tribal disputes to young and old people who wanted to use divination to see if they were going to travel out of Nigeria or make it big and earn a lot of money to feed their families. I was competing with all these factors, and worse still, I always felt like the outsider as I did not speak Igbo. Although I loved Bunny, sometimes it was lonely living there with him.

Claira's shrine members Asaba

# CHAPTER 27

# FINAL REGISTRY OFFICE WEDDING TRIP

"What are you wearing, Bunny?"
"The grey jeans, but I don't think they are dry."

It was 7:30 a.m., July 17th 1997, and Bunny and I were preparing for our trip to Akukwu Igbo to register our wedding at the office and collect the formal wedding certificate vital for both my passport and his visa.

I would indeed be marrying my own prince twice, as we had already had a tribal marriage, but it was all about us complying with visa and passport requirements. We had been informed that we needed to take two witnesses, one male and one female. Bunny had asked Obi, a student of his who was learning the oracle, but Obi hadn't turned up the day before to confirm. So, I had invited Ojo, the Rasta musician who was staying with us for a couple of days. The more the merrier, as far as I was concerned, and much better to have more than the two required witnesses than to find ourselves a witness short!

Marianna, a young Christian lady who had begun to call and clean the house, was to be my female witness. She was twenty-five years of age, a small, pretty demure little girl who was keen to travel to Italy at some point. Marianna got on very well with Ojo because she loved singing. I felt it was very important that we were all friends with one another, considering the arduous journey we were to embark on. They were required by law to know Bunny and I as our witnesses, so we felt happy with them both, knowing this was the case. Although it was not very far in miles, it was an awkward place to get to and involved at least a bus, a car, and a motorcycle to get there—and a lot of hassle.

Ojo was in the lounge, trying to dry his jeans out via the steam iron without much success. I entered the lounge, feeling sorry for him trying to manage as the jeans were very damp. "Ojo, I have some red jeans I think will fit you. Do you want to wear them?" I asked.

"Well, yes, I think so. Let's see them first," said Ojo. I fumbled through my suitcase and threw them to him. He was a similar build to Bunny and approximately a size 32 jean. Luckily for him, they fitted perfectly. Then in walked Bunny, wrapped in only in a bath towel. Now he needed sorting out; he also had wet jeans. Ojo rushed off to the shop to purchase some bread for breakfast. He was excited with his bright new outfit.

"I could have worn those red jeans," said Bunny childishly.

"Well, here I am with two Rastas without a pair of jeans between them It's ridiculous, Bunny," I said laughingly.

"I don't know what I'll wear now," said Bunny, not appreciating the joke.

"Why not wear the grey trousers that we both wore in the Gambia, Bunny? I suggested, hoping desperately to get him sorted out quickly so I could go and have my shower!

"Sue, go and take your bath. We will sort it all out later," said Bunny in his fatherly tone.

I sometimes felt like a wardrobe mistress, sorting Bunny out. He never knew what to wear until the very last moment.

By 10:00 a.m. everyone was washed and dressed, and Marianna had arrived, looking really lovely in a white Muslim-type outfit complete with headdress. We set off walking, and the two men lagged behind, speaking to all the neighbours in the usual African friendly manner. Marianna and I walked ahead, engrossed in each other's conversation and only giving polite nods to neighbours. The sun shone brightly as we made our way to the busy expressway to start catching our vehicles, which Ojo had flagged down from the expressway. As each vehicle arrived, Ojo and Bunny started the African hassle on prices, where the drivers would verbally argue over a few naira. Just before we left the red dusty road towards the taxi area, Obi, Bunny's student, joined us midway, obviously keen to be involved in such a happy day. When we reached Akukwu Igbo, Bunny and Ojo asked Mariana, myself, and Obi to wait in the town centre whilst they went ahead to the offices to negotiate the price for the much-needed wedding registration certificate.

It's always difficult to negotiate when something is so valuable to you, and although the receipt said 200 naira, we had to pay 2,000 naira, as this, I was told, was the bribe expected to get what we wanted. As if that wasn't bad enough, we had to wait two hours whilst all staff attended a meeting. How inefficient, I thought, does the whole business of registration for birth, marriages, and deaths have to stop because of a meeting? Sometimes the African ways made my blood boil, but Bunny politely reminded me that anger doesn't work with these people, as they'd just get stroppy and tell you to come back in two weeks' time.

Eventually a young man started writing the marriage certificate by hand, and Bunny, myself, Mariana, and Ojo waited silently to sign. In England, this would be done in the privacy of the church. I imagined my father and the best man looking on, whilst my mother waited in the church, dressed in her finery with a grandiose wedding hat. How far removed from all that this makeshift wedding seemed. I felt a twinge of sadness as I fantasised how lovely it would be for Bunny and me to get a church blessing in England.

When it became time for signatures, I felt myself panic. I realised I would have to sign it with my new name, but I'd not practised my new signature yet. I printed it almost childlike and felt annoyed with myself for not practising it well. A small obnoxious little man in a shiny brown suit led us all to the registrar's office. With a rude attitude, he presented the three handwritten copies to the registrar, who was a rotund man in a safari suit who wore a solemn face full of officialdom and he was obviously very aware of his power and influence.

He raised his head and said, "Is this you, Susan Elizabeth Hadley?"

"Yes, it is," I replied

"Is this you, Bunny Ugochukwu Anikwe?"

"Yes, sir," replied Bunny.

"Are you Ojo? And this is Marianna? The witnesses?" he asked.

"Yes, sir, we are," they replied in unison.

"How well do you know this couple, Ojo?"

"I know them very well, sir. They are already like husband and wife to me," said Ojo.

"And you, Marianna, how well do you know this couple?"

"Very well, sir. They are like husband and wife to me also," said Marianna.

"Marianna, how well do you know this man Ojo?" asked the registrar.

"Oh, I know him very well, sir," replied Marianna humbly.

It was getting a little like an interrogation, so I decided to lighten the atmosphere a little by adding a bit of humour. I looked towards the registrar and said, "Actually, Ojo would like to know Marianna much better."

It worked! There was a roar of laughter, and the registrar proceeded to stamp the certificates and wish us a happy married life together.

We started to leave the room, but Bunny stayed behind to speak to the registrar personally. I peeped round the door to see Bunny just removing his hat. The two men looked at one another for a few seconds, and then the registrar recognised Bunny and their faces both changed with a smile of recognition. They spoke quickly in Illah language and then stood up to shake hands. Apparently, the registrar knew Bunny's father very well, and he was also an African traditionalist who owned his own shrine locally, Bunny informed me.

It seemed in my experience of visiting the businessmen there in Nigeria, they all made a great display of being a Christian with Jesus Christ trinket displayed everywhere, plus their Christian wedding photographs, so it was unusual to see no trinkets. The registrar looked over in my direction and again wished me a long and happy marriage and a safe journey to England.

Another task was done, so we were yet another step closer to our goal. We would soon be on our way to England. I hoped that Bunny's visa would be allowed, that we would have enough money to do what we needed to do, and that we could travel together. Slowly but surely, we were getting closer to having all the documentation for Bunny's departure to visit England.

I had been struggling to live there without any help from home and getting money from England into Nigeria was very difficult. We arranged eventually for a friend of a friend from the UK, who was travelling out to Nigeria on business, to loan us some money. I was hoping that we could keep earning so that we could at least buy some presents for my family (as I felt it was only fair, considering how much they'd supported me on this adventure).

But the shrine business was getting increasingly quiet. Most of Bunny's clients seemed to be coming from a nearby village called Abavo. Not much in the way of Agbor business these days. We felt that Agbor was rich with Christians and Muslims and that it was only the older generation that seemed to be using the old tribal medicines and customs. Bunny constantly worried about this and felt that he needed to attract more business locally. But a lot of the preachers locally were against the Christians using the shrine as they felt this was the devil's work. So, we had a lot of distrust and superstitions around the religion. I could not find any books written that were anything like as strong as the Bible or the Koran.

It seemed the religion was handed down through the generations by storytelling and word of mouth. My thoughts raced ahead as we travelled together.

We arrived home to Agbor tired and dusty, broke but happy. Again, I was reminded that any sign of something being important and where a white lady is involved would certainly double any costs daily for Bunny, and that continued to worry me as I didn't wish to be a burden to him and his family.

Now home, we showered then and entered the shrine. Back to business, I thought. No shaking off the confetti and travelling off into the mist on our honeymoon.

Bunny dressed tribally after the wedding

# CHAPTER 29

# DR. NWAOMU AND THE MORTUARY

"**B**unny, I need to call my mother. Where else can I go to use the phone? Is there anywhere else besides that local post office?"

In the 1990s there in Nigeria, I saw no sign of a mobile phone, and only if you were rich did you have a landline.

"You could ask Dr. Nwaomu. After all, you know him well enough now, and he is a good friend," replied Bunny.

"You need to give me some naira to pay him then. Is that OK?"

Bunny passed over some money, and I started to make my way to his clinic on foot to save money.

Rainy season was upon us and the rains had begun; the red dusty roads in Agbor were awash with large boulders and massive holes, so I had to walk very carefully, avoiding the hazards of Agbor traffic plus loose animals. These included wild pigs, chickens, and goats running to cross the roads. Dr. Nwaomu was always a delight to visit, and recently he had requested an A4-size photograph of me to hang in his surgery. Always joking, he said that he hung it there so he could say he had a white patient whom he wanted to be his girlfriend. I liked his sense of humour, but it was still weird seeing my photo on his wall!

The doctor had more girlfriends than I cared to remember. He'd divorced several years before I met him, and his family were grown up now, so he was enjoying life, I guess!

He was a strong atheist who didn't believe in what he called "all this religion nonsense." Despite his distaste for any religion, he still enjoyed spending time with us, knowing Bunny was a chief priest. The doctor would often call around the house with Jackie, his nurse, and drink Chelsea gin or cola with us. I'd noticed recently that my green skirt from Wallis was beginning to hang loose around my waist; plus, I was beginning to worry about such a large weight loss. I hadn't had a period for over eight weeks and thought I was suffering from anorexia nervosa again, or perhaps I could even be pregnant. I was secretly hoping I'd get chance to discuss this with him on my visit.

On arrival, I was greeted by Jackie, his nurse who was a friendly lady with family in the village of Agbor. Jackie was loyal, and helpful and always spoke very good English; she led me through the surgery into the consulting room. The doctor was always pleased to see me and happy to make time for me without an appointment. After an initial catch up, I finally got around to asking him if there was any chance I could use his landline to phone home. Unfortunately, he told me that the phone in the surgery was only for local calls. I was getting homesick again.

He sensed my disappointment and jokingly, said, "Now, would you like to see the room at the end? It's even called 'The End.'"

It was a mortuary that he owned. As his practice was on the main road, he took a lot of trade. He joked, "They say people die daily, and are born daily."

He laughed out loud, and his large chest heaved up and down as that sparkle in his eyes twinkled.

"Come and see; don't be afraid." Reluctantly I stepped forward into that room, and instantly the smell of formaldehyde assaulted my nose. Rows and rows of trays held naked dead bodies. I had never witnessed such a place. The bodies varied in colour from blue to grey. I commented on this, and he informed me that some had been dead longer than others.

"They have to have the main artery at the top of the leg injected to preserve them," he commented as he held up the machinery.

"Why is that?" I said.

"It's to preserve the body for when the funeral takes place. Plus, we have to put make-up on them so that they look nice. They soon begin to deteriorate here in this heat if I am not careful."

The stillness and smell made me feel nauseous.

"So, this is where I will finish up if I don't get well in the hospital here, then?" I said.

"Ha-ha! You won't know about it, so don't worry," he joked. "I hear non-Christian kings bury their wives under the floorboards in the house anyway, so watch out, Sue."

I laughed as we walked slowly out of "The End" room, glad to be getting out alive!

The doctor had had a busy day, as during the night armed robbers had caused an accident, which involved some farmers returning from the fields on the expressway. The doctor had been busy sewing limbs back onto the dead corpses to make the poor unlucky victims look as best he could for when their grieving families arrived.

In Africa I felt I was living so near life and death. The roads were so dangerous during the day and even more so at night, when there were no roadside floodlights to help people see where they were going.

Whilst with the doctor, I took the opportunity to question him about my lack of menstrual periods, and he asked if I had been suffering from fainting and if I had gone off my food or even started eating strange mixtures of food. Funnily enough, I'd been eating tomatoes as if they were going out of fashion. He said to give it a while longer; then we could think about doing a pregnancy test.

"Pregnant" …" pregnant"—the word buzzed through my head. That's ridiculous. I'm too old for all this. I would surely need to go home if that were the case, as we could not afford the medical fees in Africa.

The sweat trickled down my back as I picked my way back across the red dirt tracks home even more carefully than when I had arrived, just in case.

A cockerel squawked near me, and five baby chicks pecked away at the rubbish in a pile near the river. New life, eggs, chicks, and babies. Was it a sign? I wondered.

I travelled back to our compound. Bunny lay sleeping as the sun pounded down on our bedroom. It was so hot in there as the fan never seemed to work properly. He was still dressed in his white robes; he must've been tired not to have got undressed. I wiped the sweat from my brow, washed my feet outside on the porch using a plastic kettle, as I had seen so many Gambians do, stripped down to my underwear, and lay down and dozed next to him.

I began praying that I could hold a child in my womb for nine months and actually conceive. In my past I had previously suffered with endometriosis, which meant I had never actually managed to conceive. I had been told by a specialist back in 1976 that it was highly unlikely that I would ever conceive, so I'd never dared to think any different for fear of disappointment. But now I really wanted to conceive the heir to Bunny's kingdom. As boy children were considered special amongst the tribes, then suddenly nothing would be too much trouble for me in all his homes and towns. I also felt that Bunny would maybe not stray or take another wife if I had a child and an heir. If this did not happen, I also had been prepared, since we met, that one day he would take a second or third wife and that this would be the natural, tribal, old-fashioned Igbo way. After all, his father, the king, had over fifteen wives in his life and ten living children.

I felt a lot of pressure was upon me as a woman to conform to this way of life, as I feared I may let him down, perhaps, if I should stay as his barren wife.

Bunny woke as a loud pig startled us, snorting outside our compound window.

"Hi, Sue, how did you get on at the doctor's?"

"Not bad...he wants to check me in a few weeks concerning my lack of periods."

"Does that mean you are with child, my dear wife?"

"We will know in the future. Bunny, if I am not with child, is everything OK with us? I did tell you when we met that I am past childbearing age, honey."

"Sue, there are many children here whose parents would love their child to be ours and to be brought up as a king-to-be, so do not worry, darling."

"You mean they would hand him over to be raised by us?"

"Of course. It would need to be a light-brown child, but he would be well fed and educated and have a great life and still be able to see his parents, so it is fine."

"This is not how it is in England, Bunn we have to adopt formally. I need to think about it all."

"We can discuss this in the future. Do not concern yourself," he said.

"I am a young man with a big future ahead of me and a lot of things to cover first. Oh, now what's happened to that girl whom I sent to the market for my rice?"

The moment had passed; it was obviously now time for beans and rice! The light streamed in as Bunny opened the door and stepped out to shower.

Doctor Nwaomu & Jackie, his nurse (left of him)

# CHAPTER 30

# SHRINE MISDEMEANOUR, AGBOR

Over twenty people were now living with us in our compound in the August of that year, mostly customers and family, and Bunny and I were organising the building of large iron gates to be fitted for security; plus we had a large wall built around the shrine to give us more privacy from the neighbours. This was taking a lot of money that I was having sent from the last of my savings from home. The huts around the shrine at the back were getting full.

After worrying last month about the shrine business being quiet, Bunny was now constantly on call with his chief priest duties. Many came to see his white wife from England and Bunny. He said that since being married, he had received more customers. The only problem was there being so many mouths to feed. There were shrine workers and patients and family; now I never had less than six or seven to feed.

When we had arrived in Umudein Street, Agbor, Francis was helping the chief priestess to look after Bunny's father's shrine. He was a tall, brusque man with a booming voice. He lived at the back of the shrine in one of the concrete huts that overlooked the inner courtyard, and before coming to live at our compound, he was by profession a driver and a farmer. He had become the alpha male whilst Bunny had travelled out to the Gambia. He had a bossy manner and a loud voice. But I must say he had done a good job keeping everything tidy in Bunny's absence, but unfortunately, the shrine hadn't attracted many new people. But with respect to him, he had kept things tidy there; he might have even put some people off. He wouldn't tolerate fools gladly, and he would often quarrel with the seven women who swept the shrine and chalked the floors in that holy place. Not that the maintenance took long, as the inner sanctum was no bigger than a garden shed, but its cleanliness mattered. It was painted white and had many pots, ornaments, voodoo symbols, and containers stored there.

Some effigies lay on the floor, and various items stored in bottles that always reminded me of Dandelion & Burdock pop. Kola nuts lay around. A large piece of string hung at the back with dead baby-chick carcasses. They had been hung by their feet for two days as sacrifices to the tutelary gods. Gin and a couple of razors were stored for tribal marking of the followers with the mark on their chest and upper back. The mark resembled an egg timer but had great meaning spiritually. Although Bunny had often said that "razoring" or tribal markings were all part of their tradition. Africans would then also know which tribe each person was from. The markings would often be done by a chief priest or chief priestess in their town. Bunny said that his face had been razored to show he was an Igbo man, and this was a big part of their tradition. Often people would ask if I wanted to be marked, but somehow this did not appeal to me. Even if I did have tribal markings put on my face, I was not a black Igbo person externally even if I felt like one within. So, I politely turned the offer down whenever it was mentioned at events. I laughed when I thought how much the British and Europeans spend on having creases and marks removed from their faces and that to inflict the pain and the scarring on one's face voluntarily was not my cup of tea. Although I did think about people who had tattoos put on in the UK and abroad and thought, maybe we are not so different after all. But having it done with just a swig of native gin was not for me. Many beliefs my people had would differ, but overall, I felt we had more in common as a nation with Africans than we had differences. Tribal beliefs are so ingrained that I often thought that it was not my place to try and change these, and what harm did they do anyway.

During our stay, Francis tried to continue to rule the compound, but everyone now knew the chief priest Ugo (Bunny) was back home. Bunny had a lot of authority and power in Awucha shrines. His father had created a good following, and Bunny had been trained well by his father but things were awkward.

With his loud voice, Francis would think nothing of bellowing to passers-by in the street near our bedroom door at 5:30a.m. He once even tried to come into our room, after banging on the door, because of some annoyance he felt. Unfortunately, he was now feeling the effect of Bunny returning and was frustrated by the attitude of the seven women who served the shrine, who were becoming restless living with two bosses. He was struggling to control them, because he was losing their respect. He never performed any spiritual events or did much in the way of divination, so the women were becoming frustrated with the fact that he expected to be waited on and fed up to five times a day. He spent the long hours between tribal events with his girlfriend, who lived near the shrine, and the women seemed to dislike his promiscuity. There were rumours that he had already left his wife in the village, and his children were hungry.

We awoke one morning to hear that Francis had been taken to hospital from his girlfriend's house with what sounded like a slipped disc in his back. However, Awucha followers said that maybe he had been cursed and wondered whether he was responsible for the money that had gone missing from the shrine. No one was sure of this, but many would say that the gods had cursed him with a big illness.

We later heard that Francis had sadly died of his back complaint and that on his deathbed he had asked for the gods to forgive and heal him. Many followers in African tribal religion have very high values; for example, they often don't drink much (except hot gin at ceremonies), so any breaking of their standards, such as womanising, drinking, theft, or ill treatment of their wives and families was very much frowned upon.

The Agbor chief priestess was performing rituals and healing the and sick. So, she used to hide the money in the deepest part of the shrine. As everyone is quite suspicious of the shrine, no one wants to steal money from this sacred and holy place, as they fear for their lives—even if they get away with the crime somehow, they will meet an ill fate. At night the praying, dancing, chatting, and singing would begin. The totem in the middle of the yard had large African snails hung up by string.

Everyone started arriving dressed in white and greeted each other. The women came with their babies strapped on their backs. All were welcome. Each had their own reason and need for being there. The drumming and symbol playing would begin, and everyone danced. A trance-like state was achieved in that shrine by dancing round and around, some had fits and began prophesying. I never seemed to have any trance states myself, although my dreams seemed to be getting more spiritual. The chief priestess had asked the shrine if Francis had taken their money, but I could not understand from the loud discussions if they actually clarified that. Because he had taken ill so suddenly after this event, they seemed to assume that the shrine was punishing Francis, but really, I think that incident could well remain a mystery. Soon after all this, everyone stopped talking about it, but it still to this day remains a mystery in my mind.

In order to get over our problems, we travelled around the shrines in the area to see how the Tribal Religion was fairing over the next few weeks. I sat in the shrine of Augustine a friend of Bunny's and after this photo was taken I had a massive headache as no camera had ever flashed in that old shrine.

Augustine and I in his father's shrine.

Awucha Chief Priest in Agbor

Ras Bunny Ugochukwu
Born with the gift of a seer
African tradition now your way
A musician priest, prince of all
White robes sway around you
Long dreadlock's in your hair
Mixing your herbs and medicines
Ancient rituals and cures administered
Many believers visit and pray in hope
Answerable only to the spirits
You spit out your food first to the gods
Honouring all the advice and help
Wise in your ways you share your power
A light to all who visit the shrine.

CHAPTER 31

# IDEHI EPHOD OF THE KING

May, and it seemed all too soon that the rainy season had begun, but it seemed never ending. The lightning flashed into our room, waking us both. I gripped Bunny tightly as the noise was deafening. I wondered when it would stop. Even the wild pigs who usually grunted outside our bedroom window at night had been beaten off by the strong downpour. As we arose, the women in our compound were already sweeping the porch and laying chalk on the entrance to the shrine in the yard. It was environment day in the town of Agbor, so everyone was making their homes and gardens look clean.

"Bunny, don't forget I'm visiting your father today in Illah to work on my diary with him. I feel the need to see him urgently," I said as Bunny was dressing.

"I know you mentioned it. How long will you stay?" he asked.

"Probably overnight and then come back the next day."

"Oney should go with you, Sue, to show you the way, as you will not be able to find the house alone, I think."

"Yes, I will. Just give me the address, Bunn. It's OK," I said.

Really, I was still maintaining my independence, which was sometimes difficult in Nigeria, especially being the white wife of an African prince and chief priest. To be truthful, I really enjoyed visiting Illah to see the king and was looking forward to the adventure, but I felt tense about this visit for some reason. Always Bunny sent an escort with me, and this would mean double the cost for him for our transport.

The rains persisted that morning, and I had just finished packing my overnight bag when I was surprised to see a figure had arrived at our door—one of Bunny's younger brothers, Nnamdi (his name means "my father is still alive".

Only sixteen, and shorter in height than his older brothers, such a lovely boy, but he looked so sad that day and a little lost. His head hung down as he passed my porch. Apparently, he had travelled from Illah, having just left the king's bedside.

"Hello there! I was just coming to see you and your father," I said.

I was surprised to see him standing there on our steps.

"My father is sick. Where's Ugo?" he replied quickly.

"In the shrine," I said.

Nnamdi slowly walked to the shrine; his head was bowed, and he seemed deep in thought. There was something final about this visit. It was almost as though the king had sent him to make sure that before his own demise, he saw everyone.

I didn't know what to do, so I started to tidy our bedding.

Bunny entered our room, looking very solemn.

"My father is very ill, Sue. You must go and represent me until I can get there, as I must finish my shrine work. I am not coming yet. It is not time."

"Bunny, I think you will regret not visiting this time, because it may be your last chance. I am very psychic, and I can feel it, honey." I knew that it was this feeling of urgency and angst that very morning that had urged me to get to Illah.

But Bunny was adamant that he needed to sort his people out in the shrine first.

Once word had got around, it felt like all the people in our compound were leaving to visit the king, apart from Bunny.

The king's first wife was already boarding a local bus, leaving her family in our compound, in order to be at his bedside. The wives would now all come together—first, second, and third wife—forgetting their differences in this time of worry over the king's health. The king's popularity as a chief priest and practitioner of herbal medicine and divination was well known, it seemed, in Delta State. Many of his wives had now died, but his children and extended family were still immense. As he owned twelve shrines, he had a great following of people there as many people who worshipped the gods at the shrine or had been healed by Bunny's father.

The rain beat down on the red sand in the yard. The heavy rain was almost deafening as it splattered down from the tin roofs and then ran along the guttering into all our large plastic water containers. These containers were for our drinking and bathing water, so the rain was vital for us. Oney stirred from his room in the compound and started packing to leave for Illah.

A verbal silence prevailed that day; it felt as though the very man who had built his Awucha tribal empire was perhaps leaving this world to enter into a new life very soon.

"Here, take a thousand naira and give it to my mother. Also, take three hundred naira for your fare money and spending money. Is that OK?" said Bunny.

"Yes, that will be fine," I said.

I placed the money carefully in my bag as Bunny watched; then he kissed me long and lovingly on the mouth.

Oney was standing with a large black umbrella, waiting to accompany me, looking forlorn.

Bunny and Black Moses, our musician friend, would wrap things up in Agbor and then travel to join us all.

Oney and I jumped into a taxi for our sombre journey. Everything was moving the same—people were going about their business and jumping on motorcycles. Agbor, a town of mosquitoes and motorcycles, was busy. Children were running in the streets, and women were shouting as they greeted each other on their porches. Little boys kicked tin cans and old footballs to each other or fought over bicycles; goats bleated in the streets untethered as they ate the rotten vegetation.

After one hour we were there. I was not armed emotionally for what was to greet me. I entered papa's bedroom. The king was almost like a shell of his former self. He had lost so much weight. When I last saw him, he was in a four-poster bed. This had been replaced by a single bed, but he couldn't even sit up in that now, as he lay prostrate, weak, and helpless.

"Sans teeth, sans eyes, sans everything," went through my mind (the seven stages of man).

My mother-in-law sat crying, wearing dirty clothes, which indicated that she'd not left his side for many days. The king's lungs were in a state of collapse, and I could hear the gurgling noise of the bronchitis and pneumonia that riddled his body. The left side of his body was paralysed from the stroke he had suffered seven years ago, at the age of ninety.

I leant over the bed and where his face was turned towards me.

"Hello, Papa. We came as soon as we heard. It's such a long way to see you," I whispered.

I noticed his beautiful eyes had acquired a grey tinge to them. He focused on me and said, "N'dow" (an Igbo greeting for hello).

"N'dow," I replied.

I do believe that was the last word he ever spoke before he was ready to join the spirit world. He was fading fast or some would say transfiguring before our very eyes, and nothing it seemed could stop this deterioration.

The day passed quietly. The women took it in turns to massage his neck, face, and back with some herbal medicine that looked like a brown paste containing oil.

At around 5:00 p.m., he really started to get very ill. He had started to vomit and have spasmodic fits that completely shook his body. Many of the women began to cry out loud. I knew somehow that he could hear everyone speaking—it seemed that he was conscious but was already in the realms of the spirit world. The women told me it was the shrine's powers keeping him alive. His body shook with pain as he convulsed, and it was horrible to watch.

The next morning the eldest children of the king continued to light the bamboo-and-wood fires in front of the house in order to make breakfast and to obtain hot water for bathing.

The third-eldest brother of Bunny's, called Sunday, was a very tall, commanding person. He had arrived from Asaba, a town nearby. Sunday called me aside from the bedroom for a family discussion. I recounted the history of the king's illness and all that the women had done to help the king, but Sunday was not happy. He really was grief stricken and wanted to save his father.

"Has he seen a doctor?" he asked.

"Someone called a doctor, but your mother said he didn't come," I replied.

"Well, perhaps they did not speak to the doctor properly and explain what is wrong," he replied, and Oney nodded in agreement as he sat next to Sunday.

"Come on then, let's go and find the nearest and best doctor then," I said.

"Sunday, what do you think?" asked Oney.

"I think we should not waste time. Let's go now," replied Sunday.

"There is no phone here. We must walk quickly into the town. It's not too far. Come," Oney replied.

"Yes, come, Sue. We know where the doctor's place is. Follow us," Sunday said.

We said our goodbyes, and Sunday explained to his mother, who was both queen and chief priest's wife, just where we were going and that we would get help.

Now the white man's medicine would need to intervene. I wondered how his wives would react. Also, maybe the king in his life had always relied on traditional herbal remedies. In the back of my mind, I was confused between a third-world perspective and a first-world one. Was I African or English? At this point I wondered. But if my ways would help, and I had some money with me, this was expected and I felt it was the right thing to do to save such a great man. We almost ran to that white-brick building that served as a doctor's practice in Illah.

I began worrying about Bunny's reaction, whether he thought I had taken over. But it was Sunday's suggestion, and anyway, bugger it, I thought.

This man is in pain, and no one should suffer like that. It was a bit scary because the women were already weeping and doing divination to find the king's (idehi) a necklace worn around the chief's neck normally. It's a type of juju (a type of "supernatural object;" is thought to have magical powers. Often African's do wear them around their necks to ward off evil and encourage good health, good fortune, and wealth.)

Sometimes it is a kola nut mixed with many other items like a tiger's tooth, human hair, nail clippings, and other items gathered by the chief, which is then wrapped in cotton and put on a leather necklace and worn around the believer's throat. The custom goes that the king or chief priest would on his deathbed summon the eldest member of the family such as his son or a chief priestess, and they would have a private ceremony to immerse this item into water. This would then allow the person to die. They say this has to be administered to allow the chief to die as the shrine or its powers could keep him alive when it was his time to go.

We arrived at the surgery. It resembled a small concrete hut, government-type 1960s building. I asked the nurse, who was wearing a white coat, if the doctor visited homes after his surgery. She waved her arm in the direction of the doctor's private room.

Sunday, Oney, and I entered. "I'm sorry to disturb you, Doctor" I heard myself saying. The doctor rose to shake my hand. He was a young Indian man, no older than twenty-eight with a kindly face and a gentle manner. "My father-in-law is ninety-seven years of age. He is very sick with a weak heart, and he is having fits and convulsing. I know he is not one of your patients, but can you come and see him very soon? We will pay you," I blurted out, feeling very tearful. The doctor agreed to come as soon as his last patient had gone that day.

Two hours later, when the doctor arrived he administered tablets for the pain and attached a drip to the king's arm; he hooked it up to the ceiling and advised us to keep watch.

Later whilst on his way out of the door, he admitted to us that he did not hold out much hope and that probably the king's time had finally come.

He said, "He has had a long, healthy life, and I am amazed that he is ninety-seven." He bade us goodnight and disappeared into the night. I knew he was probably right that we would have only one night left.

As darkness descended, a small kerosene lamp was lit and placed in the middle of the room. I watched as it cast shadows across the walls and ceiling. The king's breathing was now very shallow.

"Can someone say a prayer in your language?" I asked.

Alice, one of his wives, began a small prayer; then one or two of the other woman joined in. His first wife sang a little song of sorrow slowly and mournfully. All the wives were united in this very sad time of his ill health. Alice was the barren wife of the king. She'd stayed as his confidant and close friend and had reared Bunny from childhood. She obviously loved the king very much, as did all the wives. Only three of the fifteen wives were left, as some had moved away or died.

I fell asleep from the heat and exhaustion, and when I woke in the morning, the king was dead. I knew this instinctively as I could hear his wives wailing and the other women sobbing. Alice wept silently near his bed. The women closed the door of his room, and I presume the wives were laying him out and dressing him in his white robes and placing his crown and feather on his hat and head.

The family then at 11:00 a.m. sat him up on top of his clean double bed with white sheets, and a white feather on his headband stood proud. I wrote this poem as I sat by his bedside, awaiting Bunny's arrival from Agbor. Many of the women and children of the village sat on an old wooden bench next to me on the porch of the king's home. Bunny had telephoned to a nearby house, and they had run and told him. Bunny was now travelling back to us with Black Moses. We heard the cannon being fired to honour the king in the distance. I sat by his bed alone and wrote this poem.

Chief and King of Illah

## Great Chief

Great chief, in state you lie
White clothes cover you
As on your bed you rest
Your red chief's hat and feather
You wear with pride
The cannons have been fired

News spreads quickly
Your demise is public
Illah people in their hundreds gather

I stand by your bed
Heaviness in my heart
I wished I'd known you better
Always when a hero dies

People do feel empty
Like a great vessel has left its port
Your wives now sit crying
Bunny must wear your crown

Into the realms of spirit, you go
The death masquerade has visited
Now insects sit on your bed
The bodily shell we all witness

Will now leave you and travel
As into the new life you go
I pray to God for you
My dear king and chief,

I hope you arrive safely
Handsome in death
Oh, great man we honour you

Outside, the sun shone. I wept for the king alone; then I went out into
the yard sat on a bench and waited for Bunny to arrive. One hour later
Bunny arrived, and I delivered the news about his father. He sat silently
on the king's bed, held the king's hand, and silently wept. That evening we

slept in our large bedroom in the king's house, but we were silent together. We held each other tight as we felt the whole world changing so quickly around us, and we were still newlyweds. There was nothing to say, and Bunny seemed deep in thought. He was wondering about his new role and his responsibilities.

# CHAPTER 32

# FUNERAL ARRANGEMENTS AND OBI'S CHOICE

The following morning a dry heat prevailed, which was becoming unbearable, even for the locals. The lack of trees around the king's house wasn't helping the situation; the red dust was everywhere, and it really got into all your clothes and belongings. The women had to constantly sweep the porches. All my clothes were sticking to me, and my ankles were getting very swollen as the rain had subsided and the heat rose. My responsibilities were domestic as I had to organise extra water for the toilet, as we were getting through our supplies with the house being full of family and visitors. In Illah, the toilet was a hole on a tiled floor, which you threw a bucket of water at. I was having to visit this more often than most (part of my illness) because of the constant heat.

I had asked Bunny if the women who were cooking for us could now put less chilli in my food. I needed to eat well if I was to help Bunny out with all the funeral arrangements. I was surprised at how quickly everything happens in Nigeria when a person dies. This is due to the heat and the fact that most people do not have the body put in a mortuary, as it takes time and costs quite a lot, I heard. It was so very different from England, I kept reminding myself, where we would wait up to three weeks to bury someone. At around 2:00 p.m., people started to gather in small groups to drink palm wine and chat and grieve for the loss of their king, although we generally drank palm wine between 2:00 p.m. and 5:00 p.m. most days. I thought twice about joining the groups of men gathering to drink. I felt I had to keep my wits about me and not disgrace Bunny by dancing or enjoying the very potent palm wine or even saying the wrong thing in my broken Igbo. Not that I ever had disgraced Bunny before, but it was all different now. It was all about being respectable now after the king's death, and Bunny had told me that morning that I was now to assume the role of queen, which meant I had to behave and act more serene and gracious. I decided that my broken Igbo and the palm wine might not be a good mix today and left the men to drink on their own.

A vehicle, so covered in red dust that you couldn't make out anything about the type of motor it was, arrived in our compound area. Out stepped a medium-height, slightly stocky lady, very beautifully dressed, who looked very confident and proud, perhaps a professional business woman. This was Obi, Bunny's elder sister. She said hello and spoke with such an authoritative voice. Her manner was one of someone who was about to take charge of the situation, or at least try. All the women rushed to greet her, bowing to her as she acknowledged them by gently touching their right shoulder. Bunny rose from the edge of his father's bed. He looked forlorn about his father's death. He introduced me to Obi. She spoke very good English as she addressed me.

"Hello, Sue, how are you?"

"Fine, but really upset about the king's death. I'm sorry for your loss, Obi."

"Thank you. Now, will you come with Bunny to my house here in Illah, and we can discuss what will happen next?" She was genuinely sad about losing her father, but I got the feeling she wanted to get things sorted and for things to be done her way.

We strolled with Obi about half a mile in the heat to where she lived. Half a mile used to seem no distance at all to me, but it was hard work in the intense heat. The house was so tidy, yet it seemed full of shoes and clothes and bags—all from abroad.

She followed my gaze as I looked round. She said, "I work for the airways, Sue. That's why you see so many things here. I buy and sell items as I shop around in many countries. My husband is British, like you, but he is actually in England as we speak."

I felt relieved; at last, I had someone who could speak very good English. I felt like I been starved of British conversation for so long! And another English person in the family—well that was great.

"Would you like a mineral?" she asked.

"Yes, cola please."

Bunny ordered a malt whisky, and one of Obi's daughters took cash from Obi and rushed off to buy refreshments from a local shop.

I was gasping for a drink, even though I knew the cola would be luke-warm because we'd had several power cuts recently. I'd got used to drink-ing lukewarm cola by now. It was just another part about life in Illah. All part of the ups and downs of Nigerian life.

Obi and Bunny spoke for what seemed at least an hour on what would happen next. They spoke in their native tongue, but from the little knowl-edge I had of the language and what Bunny explained later, it seemed the siblings wanted different things. Bunny wanted a traditional burial, with his father being a practitioner of tribal customs and rituals and a recognised chief priest and African tribal practitioner or, as some would say, a voodoo king. But Obi was a Christian and wanted a Christian burial, complete with grave headstone. The friction rose in their voices, but then Bunny stood up and said that as eldest son, he would be making the decision.

We shook hands with Obi and made our way back to the king's quar-ters, keeping the invitation open for Obi to see us later and inviting her to the celebrations. Obi had changed religion a long time ago and never turned up to dance with the women anymore. It seemed to me that many young people were taking up Christianity and turning away from the old religion. Bunny would need to market his religion strongly if he were to keep it alive.

Often the Africans quoted from the Bible that they had studied, I noticed.

The Christians had taught them many things, but not all wanted to practise the Christian way of worship within the Awucha sect. In Bunny's view Jesus Christ was a prophet, but he told me that ATR believers wor-shipped God directly. And this is the way his father would have wanted things. This was my very first witnessing of how the religions divided people there, and often, the only way you realised what religion people where was upon death, as each religion had a different way of burying their dead.

I didn't see much of Obi after that. Bunny planned a traditional Awucha tribal funeral for the king. This was for people to come and grieve and celebrate his life.

We had now travelled back to Agbor in the heat. Bunny awoke from his afternoon sleep. "Well, the decision is made. We bury him tribally. It is what his people expect in Awucha religion. They will come and grieve and celebrate. You will see them coming from all over Africa as my father was a great man," said Bunny with pride as he wrapped his waist length dreadlocked hair around his head and tied it in a knot to manage it in the heat.

"Whatever you think is best, Bun," I said as I straightened the white sheet covering our bed.

It all sounded great having this big event, but I couldn't stop worrying about whether we had enough room for everyone.

"There are many rooms in my father's house," Bunny replied. "Don't worry, Sue."

Bunny told me to expect things to happen at a very fast pace. For a start, we had to sort out the funeral details post-haste; this was due to the heat and the deterioration of the body there.

Even with all the business of the funeral arrangements, Bunny was really struggling with the death of his father and was in a deep state of grief. He was quiet and spent many hours in the shrine, within the house, pondering over all his responsibilities now that he had several shrines in the vicinity to look after.

That night as I lay next to him in Agbor as he slept in his white chief priest's robe, I dreamt that his father the king's spirit was talking to me through (extra sensory perception,) and I could see his spirit moving around in a dark sludgy place full of bumps and lumps almost womb-like. He said to me "It's too bumpy in your womb. I cannot settle my spirit there."

I replied in the dream, "I know, Papa." My dream voice said, "I think it is the endometriosis causing lumps and bumps in my womb. So maybe if I eat well and try harder to get pregnant, you can visit me again."

But the dead king was drifting away as I spoke. I felt wet tears running down my face, and my sobs woke me up. I crept out of bed, left the bedroom, walked over to the wooden porch, and wept.

It was three thirty in the morning, and all I could hear was the chirp of the male crickets making a croaking sound as they rubbed their little wings together to attract the females. I felt lonely and barren. Was I ever going to be a full woman? How would my position be there if I were to not conceive?

It was a full moon and beautifully light and serene. I looked down the compound at the large banana plant and the alleyway into the courtyard of the shrine. I gazed at the places where the women hung their washing out, and my eyes fell on the water troughs made of blue-and-black plastic from the marketplace; I felt seriously homesick. Homesick enough to leave Bunny and try and distract myself from all the loss.

I still had dysentery and thought it was because I had eaten rice that was two days old. I rushed to the toilet and watched the geckos (small little lizards) scurrying up the walls as I smelt the cesspit. It was weird that they saw everything every time I went into that place.

The only way we had of keeping that toilet clean in Agbor was to throw a bucket of water down it as hard as possible. So, I rushed to the water trough to fill up my bucket, and I tried to do this as quietly as possible so as not to wake all my family and friends in the compound. By now we had up to ten people living there.

I also felt strange inside my tummy, as if something had moved, or maybe I should consider myself pregnant. I did not know. I had never been pregnant, and I longed for the English technology and the *National Health Service* that could easily tell me what had happened. Or had I just imagined it all?

I thought about mine and Bunny's last conversation before he had fallen asleep, as he was worried about his father's reputation and how he could rise to the challenge of being the new king and chief priest. I wanted to help to bury the king formally. I knew his spirit was watching over us and that I should look after Bunny and this family, but I was yet to think of how to do this. Everything was always about money there; it seemed to solve everything.

Logically speaking, Bunny and I needed to formally bury the king as this was expected of the eldest son. The locals thought because he had a white wife from England, we could magically make this money appear for a grand funeral lasting several days. But I was a working-class girl from humble roots myself. But according to the locals there, there was a long-held belief that of course everyone who came from England had money.

I was to hear that the custom in Nigeria was that there are two types of burial. The first occurs within days of the death of a person due to the heat, and the second is the formal burial where there is much merriment and dancing, and they cook goat's stew and rice. Also, a cow is sacrificed if the man or lady is famous or important, and many people attend. It's the custom that they drink native gin and beer and dance into the night to honour the gods and give the person a good send-off into the afterlife.

I knew we could not afford this yet, but I knew if I went home, I could raise the money to help Bunny and his family with this task. I washed my hands in the warm rainwater from the bucket and crept back into our room to be with Bunny.

It is only fair that I explain the type of religion I witnessed there in Agbor so that you can fully imagine my life. When questioning Bunny about his religion I asked him, "Do you believe that people go to heaven when they die in your African tribal religion Bun?"

"We believe in our ancestors being very good, and so it is that they will come back and enter the body of a new baby in that family. So, if you get pregnant, my father will enter your womb and be reborn." Heck, I had just dreamt that, so I was beginning to feel confused and wondered when exactly during the pregnancy (if it ever happened) would this wondrous event occur.?

I had read in the library during my time in Agbor a quote from Richard Okafor (1994) that said that *Onye a aghachighetta* (he or she has come back to life); hence the name Onochie means "he or she." Heck, I thought, is this going to happen to me? According to the author Omabala Aguleri in his book *Igbo History Hebrew Exiles or Eri*,

Igbo religion begins with the belief and worship of Chukwu or Chikudu (the great god) Chineke or Chuckwu Okilke (the creator of all things). Ani (the earth goddess) is the most important deity in Igbo social life. Any great offence is against the earth and any custom is covenant of the earth. "Odi-na-na," that is what people do or what happens in the locality of the people's land.

There was a lot to learn about the African tribal religion, but I knew I could always ask Bunny if I felt confused.

# CHAPTER 33

# IGBO COFFIN TRAIL

As we had now returned to Illah to sort things out after our brief trip back to Agbor. I felt this brief interlude had given Bunny time to sort things out mentally. I was resting in the afternoon from the heat, lying on the bed, when there was gentle knock on the door of our room there in Illah.

It was Juliet, a young girl there. She brought in an omelette with red chillies, some local bread, plus a bottle of water. Bunny was up. I could hear him on the palace porch, talking in Igbo to his mother.

There seemed no formality about death there. I noticed that no one printed it in the paper, and no registration was signed at the Registrar's Office for Births, Marriages, and Deaths. It could be described as almost an anonymity about life in Africa; one could live and die and somehow miss the system.

Bunny walked in, dressed in Western clothes complete with leather sandals and holding a leather hand pouch containing what little money we had left. He sat on the end of the bed and shared my food.

"We need to go back to Agbor and buy a coffin, Sue."

"OK, so how do we get it delivered here? I'm guessing there's no funeral director service here or anything, like in England?"

"Simple, we strap the coffin to the car. Can you be ready in ten minutes while I say goodbye to some of my chiefs?"

"What? Oh well, I've never been coffin shopping before," I said light-heartedly, but Bunny was not amused. It seemed we had to do it fast as the body of the king would lie in state for only two or three days.

The car bumped up and down the red dusty roads. We had no air conditioning and just one small bottle of water. Bunny talked about his new responsibilities and how things would change; the whole situation was getting too much. Was I ready to stand by his side and take the helm? One hour or so later, as the heat was rising, we arrived in Agbor and drove straight to a ramshackle stall in the marketplace. There were a range of coffins displayed, just as if they were tables in a furniture store! And in all sizes, all styles—from highly polished mahogany to simple pitch pine ones.

Bunny picked a simple one and bartered the price from 15,000 naira to around 10,000, which is about £50. We then dropped the back seat of the car and pushed the coffin in, strapping it in with a piece of old rope. Imagine driving through the UK like that! The whole thing was so bizarre.

Bunny stopped the car to buy a bottle of native gin. He sipped it and bought me a coke. We drove back to our compound in Umudein Street, Agbor, to gather some fresh clothes, shower, and prepare for the trip back, complete with the coffin.

After eating rice and pounded yam prepared by the women of the shrine, we got back into the car again. A silence had befallen the king's shrine in Agbor.

Bunny informed me that all the worshippers were preparing to leave their other shrines in the local towns and villages to see their tribal king lying in state and to give their condolences.

We tried to drive carefully down the bumpy, uneven roads, but it wasn't easy, and often the coffin would start sliding out. The potholes were enormous, and there were almost no traffic signals anywhere. We just had to keep beeping the horn and keep our wits about us! We had given up pushing the coffin in the back of the estate car as it slid all over the place, so now Bunny and I had secured it with rope on the bonnet of the car. We had to keep stopping every few miles and checking the rope as we had no roof rack at all. I couldn't believe this was my real life there. Sometimes, it felt more like a comedy film. I mean the idea of rushing about buying a coffin and then delivering it yourself seemed alien to me. But we had no money, so we had to do things ourselves.

Our perseverance paid off, and we arrived before 5:00 p.m. The sun was setting, so at least it was nice and cool. This was always my favourite time of the day. It was so beautiful, and sometimes we had a slight warm wind, and everything always seemed so calm in the busy streets as people went home to eat over their open fires.

As we arrived in Illah, we noticed many people had now gathered at the king's house. A transit drove into the street with worshippers from Asaba with a poster on it that read, "Let the blood of Jesus wash over you." It seemed ironic when all the passengers were African Traditionalists, dressed in their white cloths. But in Africa, none of that seems to matter. Often people practise more than one religion and so are quite happy with this way of thinking. In fact, because there in 1997, there was very little in the way of social activity, so your religion often would become your whole way of life. It offered hope and friendship and always got people to gather together. Worshipping, dancing, healing, praying, and performing rituals for young and old was a way of life. The youths between eighteen and thirty-five often migrated abroad to seek new lives in many countries, and I wondered if the old religion would survive. Although it is widely known that as the old religion is so ingrained into the Igbo's being, they would possibly congregate and practise their religion wherever they lived in the world.

I felt really honoured to be accepted at such an occasion, being the only white person there at the great king's death, and I was allowed to share in this historical moment and share and watch and feel the very same loss that I knew they were all feeling at that time.

Two days later all the food was organised, everyone had been informed, and the tribal burial was agreed. When I awoke I could hear the ladies chatting as they shaved the heads of the last surviving three of the king's wives; apparently this custom of head shaving is a mark of respect. There was much drumming and music, and the king's coffin was carried through the town area and laid to rest very near the house. We, as family, all had to wear white a cloth around our waist and orange coral beads, which were gathered from an old tea chest in the king's house. The sons wore only the cloths, and some of the cloths were shaped in the form of a male skirt, and they were bare chested in the heat. But the women wore white cotton blouses, and the "white cloths" as we termed them and they were styled as wrappers around our waists. Ifeyinwa was translating most of the day for me as it was all moving so fast in that Igbo language with speeches and songs and drumming and rituals throughout the day.

As the coffin was lowered into the earth outside the front of the house, Bunny's mother, who now had a shaved head, had to sit opposite the coffin on the soil where they were digging, with her back to the grave digger and look away. This was an act I was told to finally turn her back on her husband and to let him go into his new afterlife experience. She stood up solemnly when the last of the soil was dropped upon the coffin and moved in her white clothes into the house to grieve with the other wives sitting on the floor. Ifeyinwa and I moved amongst the crowds and greeted people solemnly. The band had arrived with their guitars and drums at the family's request. Now time to mourn and dance.

Bunny at the King's burial in Illah

# CHAPTER 34

# MALARIA STRIKES BACK IN AGBOR

Two weeks later after we had returned home to our own compound, I woke up late in the morning. Bunny was already in the shrine, rubbing palm oil on a baby's limbs whilst the mother looked on. The little girl was struggling with some sort of rheumatism making walking difficult. Bunny would rub the oil into her limbs and try and get the child to move them. I felt giddy and faint and wondered if the dysentery had taken a hold.

I put on my white wrapper and white T-shirt and walked down the alleyway to the shrine. The lady with her child was saying goodbye, and I struggled up the two steps to get into the inner room of the shrine. There was an old single mattress there with blue-and-white striped tick covering amongst the bottles of herbal medicine. The last thing I saw was that mattress as I fainted in front of Bunny. I heard his voice crying out to quickly get water.

"Quickly get water. My wife is sick," he shouted.

The next thing I remember is being held up by three people as they dragged me, with my legs dangling, into our bedroom. The noises in my head were ringing as I went into an attack of malaria. My mind was not my own; the fever had taken a hold. The women would fade in my consciousness in and out and they seemed to be bringing pieces of lime with alligator pepper on and asking me to suck them. Then the next few days were a blur as the bowls kept arriving for me to be sick in. Africans do watch you being sick, and there is no shame in that. I kept asking them to go away and not witness me being sick, but they just stayed there and dried my hair and put wet cloths across my forehead. The noise of the malaria was giving me tinnitus; all I could hear was very loud high-pitched ringing in my ears. I was delirious, and my thoughts were jumbled as into the realm of malaria my mind was taken.

Two days later, Bunny booked a taxi for me to go to Dr. Nwaomu's private surgery. I woke up in a single bed with a drip attached to my arm, and they were administering quinine. The sickness had stopped, but the weakness, the head pounding, and the delirium had not. Ifeyinwa, Oney, and Bunny sat near my bed, asking if I needed anything, but Jackie, Dr. Nwaomu's nurse, was keeping a close eye on me throughout my visit.

She stood with a bag of blood and asked Bunny in Igbo if I would like this to keep me fresh. It is believed if you renew your blood, it will solve the malaria.

Bunny said no, as he thought I should be in England, having as much help as possible and that I was so ill, this would be the only thing that would help.

Bunny had himself had a mild attack of malaria but had managed to get through it with quinine. Africans seem to be much more immune to this killer disease. Although thousands do die, I know, and it is the bite of the female mosquito that causes this. I had no marks on my body from bites, so what had happened? Dr. Nwaomu thought I may have had cerebral malaria and possibly I would not see a bite because I could have been bitten on the head underneath my hair. I drifted off into my delirious state, where the buzzing and jungle noises seemed to flourish. My weight was dropping, and I had lost all sense of where I was. I was absolutely helpless in Africa and afraid.

I looked at the door labelled *The End* and wondered if I could get to a phone one of the days and book a flight home. This could not be *The End* for me. I had to get out of Nigeria, where Bunny and I had very little money and no real hope of me being cured.

Luckily, I pulled through that bout of malaria with Dr. Nwaomu's quinine injections and bed rest. But it had taken its toll on my health, and my weight had dropped by one stone. My clothes seemed to hang off me. Bunny and the woman of the shrine gave me alligator pepper to rinse my constant dry mouth. They then insisted that I suck more limes and drink lots of water. I don't think I had ever seen so much food. I ate yams every day and hot pepper soup, plus anything I fancied. Bunny would arrange for it to be bought, including coffee, which was really expensive there, along with condensed milk.

The women walked me to the back of the garden and would wash me down with hot and cold water as I stood facing the wall in the compound. I held onto the wall, naked with my legs apart, as they splashed buckets of hot water over me. A real make do bathroom.

Everyone was so kind. I felt I owed them my life. I was totally dependent on them all in the shrine and struggling to think straight; all I could hear was the hissing noise in my left ear, a side effect of the quinine. In fact, little did I know that this hissing and ringing noise in my left ear would last for the rest of my life!

# CHAPTER 35

# SAYING FINAL GOODBYES

Six weeks later after my slow recovery from Malaria, I made my mind up to go home temporarily to recover properly. After many discussions with Bunny about this, he finally agreed to me going home for a while. There was frantic love-making, sweating into the night, spraying our room for mosquitoes, and then sitting on our porch talking about everything that we could do to resolve the situation—but no real solution to our constant lack of money and my ill health was forthcoming.

Consequently, there was a sadness that fell between us as I repeated to Bunny that going home was the only solution for my health. A business friend from Shropshire, whom I wrote to that month telling him of my plight, offered to help me out, and very quickly he sent the money for me to get a ticket home. The ticket was very expensive from Nigeria—over £750. But I knew I could work and pay him back if I could just get well enough to board the plane.

I was feeling faint and dizzy most days and wondered if I was pregnant perhaps. Then, finally again I collapsed in the shrine onto an old mattress amongst the dead baby chicks held up by string. I heard Bunny's voice in the distance saying, "Please don't disturb my wife. She is sleeping with a sickness."

I awoke one hour later, dazed and weak. Still no period and a craving for tomatoes with salt and rice with sugar. I had to keep myself together as I packed my case slowly, noticing that all my dresses had faded. Even my underwear was a definite grey and fit only for the bin. Bunny's brothers all filed through the compound to pay their respects. I could hear their greetings as I busied myself with gathering my wash bag and tablets.

One or two people from across the village came with letters for me to post to their relatives in the UK, which I was to post when I arrived in London. Bunny and I talked of burying his father formally in the future, and of how Bunny would visit me soon in England and perhaps settle there for a while.

It was now August, and it had been two years since I had left Much Wenlock in Shropshire. I felt so different. I noticed I was speaking pidgin English. The journey by bus to Lagos had taken over six hours, and Bunny held my hand all the way, sensing that perhaps this would be difficult for us both. I had learned a new way of life. I was desperately in love with my dear Bunny, but I needed to recuperate and see my British way of life again and see my aged parents once more.

The plane had seemed full of African business people. I was the only white on the plane, not uncommon in 1997, and I really didn't want to talk to strangers. My heart was with Bunny as I thought back to the airport and how I watched him walk away. He seemed to disappear into the mass of seething bodies and beggars near the airport gate. The money changers were hassling him as he was dressed in his Western clothes. I cried before the plane lifted. We had something that we didn't want to discuss with anyone.

I had visited the toilet at the airport and felt an almighty pain across my tummy and then a terrible period. I had then watched as any hopes of our expected child fell into the water. I was motionless I knew that Endometriosis showed no mercy. This was not the first time I had major periods and was in pain. But never before had thought that perhaps I was even pregnant. Bunny was kind and said God would help us and he would pray to Awucha, his goddess.

"It's just not our time, darling," he said comfortingly as I cried on his shoulder at that airport. "I have enough children to care for with the ones my father has left, so don't worry." Any woman reading this book will know that I did worry that I could not fulfil my role as a fertile wife.

So just three hours later you would have found me listening to the shouts of the air hostess as I sat on my expensive seat on that plane to UK. I fell asleep very quickly as I sat down and did not even know the plane had ascended.

"Coffee," the air hostess shouted as the passengers held up their cups in anticipation. The tears rolled down my face onto my dress for all I had experienced there and for my loss. Coffee with real milk. Everything seemed so clean and organised on that plane—not all like my African life where I would be sweeping red dust from my porch or typing intermittently with my old word processor whenever NEPA, the electricity company, decided that there would be light. Now to sleep and forget what I may have lost and try and look forward to greeting my family back in England. Perhaps a period of convalescence would be good for me, I thought as I gazed out of the plane window.

I wondered whether I should I confide in my mother about the baby loss or not. Maybe later, I thought, as I knew she had missed me every day, and welcoming me back should be a happy time—and I didn't want to add sadness to that. Africa is hard—someone once told me—with illness, happiness, loss, gain, all being part of the adventure of falling in love in Nigeria.

After all, wasn't I part of the statistics that there were over one hundred million people living in Lagos, and every day surely children were born, and some lived, and often some died. So factually it was correct, but it did nothing to ease the pain and loss. Nothing I read about Nigeria could put this loss for me into perspective. But all this illness and loss was so overwhelming that during the flight I tried to remember all the happy times and my love for Bunny. I had to be strong for us both.

As I gazed out of the window on the plane, my mind raced back to my youth. Well, it's all about expectation. I had known in my twenties about the Endometriosis and that having a child would be difficult, if not impossible, but I'd believed deep down inside that it might be possible perhaps like many women still do and I hoped they could find a cure for this illness. But now I was very disappointed.

The English food arrived in foil trays, and a ranting and raving loud-mouthed Christian lady next to me began trying to convert anyone by reading the Bible aloud. As I was not my usual hospitable self, I moved to an empty seat on the way back from the toilet on the plane. I didn't want to offend her, but I needed to pray alone and maybe sleep before I landed.

Letter Home to Africa—Sept 1997

*My darling Bunny,*

*Good news! After only one month of leaving you, I have secured a job on the newspaper here in Oxford as a manager. It's great money, and I've have booked a flight to see you in November as I've have organised two weeks' holiday. Life is strange here in England. Am I really going to stay barren? I ask myself, but I must keep trying to get my life back on track for us, Bunny. Also, I need to earn money to help us all out, I feel.*

*We had a very big news break when I arrived. Lady Diana was killed in a car crash. The whole world is grieving. Did you see the news? My mom and I have been watching the news and reading the papers for days here.*

*But I know we have our own personal sadness, darling, but I cannot begin to worry too much now as I feel I won't function. At forty-four years of age, maybe this was my one and only chance to conceive, and this bears heavy on my heart. Such a profound double loss, especially after your father has passed. Worse still is the loss of you, my dearest Bunny. You're my life, my soulmate. I don't feel complete without you. I want you here to discuss all these big events that are happening around us.*

*I know you are praying for us, my darling. I think being sick with the water there and lack of sanitation did not help us. My only way around this has been to secure this job here in the UK and not give myself time to think about it all. Besides, we need the money, and the immigration rules say I have to have worked in a secure job for six months in order to secure the visa for you to come here to me. I feel like a fish out of water here and wonder if I did the right thing sometimes.*

*My darling, my heart is in Africa, but my body is here in England, where I feel it needs to be fully well again. The doctors are good here, and they are free! It's very confusing, because here in England my heart does ache, but my body and mind can recover from our loss.*

*I do know that I do not want to ever be hungry again, like we were in the Gambia. I have put some weight on already, and you will be very pleased with your new, plumper wife when I fly in to see you.*

*I had forgotten what a nation of retailers and shoppers we were. I realised I hadn't been clothes shopping for two years, and still my clothes were not worn out, weird huh!*

*Bunny, are you OK, my darling? Your African queen-to-be and wife misses you every day. Have you started making plans for the king's official funeral and set a date?*

*Oh, the family say hello to you.*

*All my fondest love,*

*Sue Hadley Ugochukwu Anikwe xx*

# ABINGDON IN OCTOBER 1997

After a month or so back in England, life started to take on a new routine. Just constantly working in the newspaper office was exhausting but stimulating. I longed to be back with my people in Africa. Work colleagues and family were constantly bombarding me with questions about marrying an African prince. I seemed to spend my life waiting for a letter or fax from the other side of the world.

Oxfordshire was beautiful. It seemed so clean and organised after my tribal life. But no one there seemed as friendly as the Africans towards me.

My life at the lodgings in the hotel was lonely. One of my sales girls mentioned that her friend's mom took in lodgers, so I took the telephone number and address and arranged to visit. That day changed my life as my landlady was the most joyous and welcoming person you could wish to meet—a jolly forty-five-year-old divorcee and extremely extroverted and positive. She hugged me when I arrived, which was so lovely, and as I looked around, I realised her home was spotless. I said yes to renting the smallest box room with a single bed, but it looked so lovely.

"Oh, bring your clothes in from the car!" she said.

I had rented a car for work also, so I was all set up for a working life in England. My landlady and I talked late into the night as I drank white wine with her. I was now so at home but very sad about not being with Bunny.

I have to thank her, as she encouraged me go out and dress up again. I had lost my femininity with the sadness of mine and Bunny's separation and the possible secret miscarriage. It was lovely to have someone to chat to after work, also especially when I had begun to stress with the management of the staff and the late deadlines. I was working up to sixty hours some weeks. So different from my charity work and lifestyle with Bunny.

"It's Friday," she would bellow up the stairs to me. "Come down and drink wine while we get ready to go out."

Alvera showed me all the culture and nightlife of Oxford. I needed to get out, as I still felt really lost back in England. I needed to switch off from Bunny's pleading letters for my company and money. These letters made me feel guilty and sad also. I felt guilty that his passport was not a British one and I could not afford to bring him home on that plane with me. Every day I would write my goals and try my hardest to be positive as I drove to work. My department was being worked harder and harder to make more profit.

But I had found a career again. It was so very different from sitting and meditating in Bunny's shrine in Agbor Delta State or dancing around the totem pole in voodoo style. I was so confused and not really sure where I actually wanted to be. In Africa I missed the comforts of home, but in England I missed the community of Africa.

Whilst my mother and family were glad to see me, and I enjoyed talking about Bunny when friends and neighbours asked about my African Rasta husband, coming back to England made me understand why I had left. That time away had made me remember that deep down, I had always felt I did not belong. I was just counting down the weeks until I could board that plane and go back.

# TARQWA BAY NOVEMBER 1997

S oon I was back on the plane to Africa for a holiday. I was so excited to be going there again. My new employer had agreed to honour the holidays I had already booked, so I could get back to Africa for a while. My thoughts on the plane had been all about Bunny and how I could bring him home one day. I had decided that he should see my family and maybe he could work in England and settle there for a while until his people needed him back at the shrine. Bunny had received some money from me and booked our accommodation for a real holiday.

As I arrived via boat after a long flight from England, I could not believe I was back in Nigeria. There I was in Tarqwa Bay.

"Wow, what a place, Bunny., I cannot believe you found this lovely accommodation for us!"

Bunny had used some of the money he had made from his shrine plus my money sent, to book the old hospital building for us. After my long-haul flight to Lagos and then a long bus trip and a boat trip, we had finally arrived at Tarqwa Bay. We were staring at our accommodation from a golden beach that was only a hundred yards away.

"It's a former military hospital, I think," replied Bunny. Onochie and Julie, the king's daughter from Illah, were busy carrying our bags and unpacking everything on the tiled porch. The place looked like something out of THE ENGLISH PATIENT film. A family living in the outbuilding were lighting fires with bamboo and cooking fish in the backyard area. Bunny had asked them to cook for us over their fire, and he had paid them well for the service. I carried the newly purchased mosquito nets into the rooms and proudly placed them across the beds. I definitely did *not* want malaria again!

We had so much space, as the wards were now converted into bedrooms. Bunny and I had never known air conditioning; it was a big change. We had only been able to afford one stand-up fan during our time together in the Gambia. The only drawback I could see was the lack of electricity anywhere on the island. If you purchased your own generator, then you could have the luxury of electricity, but we did not have the funds for that. The ceilings of our rooms were still a maze of steel structures, and I was informed they were used for hanging the hospital equipment and hoisting traumatised soldiers into wheelchairs. I guess they would also have been used for hanging sheets during the Second World War. The rooms seemed to go on forever, and there was a dining room still stacked full of chairs, which reminded me of a school dining hall. I joined Bunny and a fellow Rasta musician, who were speaking in English about their music. The Rasta raised his guitar, and they began singing reggae together. Oney played drums whilst sitting on the wooden bench. Memories of the flight and the noisy bus full of Nigerians en route faded. I began to relax. I had forgotten Bunny's funny habits and the smell of him. I wanted to just cuddle him all night and stroke his long dreadlocks and hear his commanding voice again. We made love whilst the fan droned above us and shadows were cast across the room from the blue mosquito net.

Then after only two nights of bliss, Bunny said, "I have to travel back to Lagos tomorrow for a couple of days." I felt my heart jump. I had been feeling very vulnerable over the past six months since leaving Bunny in Nigeria. He was a young man in his thirties, and the fact that this father had married fifteen wives over his lifetime had been playing on my mind. With a wife in England, would Bunny's heart wander? And could my heart take sharing the love of my life with another woman, or even other women?

I knew Bunny would sooner or later meet and marry one of his own tribe, an Igbo girl. And after the miscarriage, I felt sexually weak. I hadn't forgotten being called "barren" as one of the worshippers of Awucha had cruelly described me. I didn't want to feel jealous, but hey, I had invested all my money, energy, and time into the marriage, and every minute with Bunny on my holiday was precious.

"It's chief business, Sue," he said as he packed his bags to travel. "You can stay with Oney to guard you, Sue," he said so nonchalantly. He was to be gone two days concerning his kingship. The chiefs, of whom there were fifteen under him, had summoned him to discuss business in Illah.

Bunny didn't wish to be crowned yet as he considered taking his father's role as an old man's job. As a king, he wouldn't be able to work on his music and perform. Tribal kings were not allowed to work full time, he informed me. Besides, there was all the funeral business to book and see to.

I had sent Bunny the last of my savings, over £1,600, to bury the king in style, but I felt I would like to be there at the meeting.

As meetings were conducted in Igbo, it would be difficult for me to understand everything being said, unless I had someone interpreting. I decided to let go a little and just accept that this is probably how it's going to have to be from now on. It was such a shock after being in charge of all areas of my life as a liberated single woman in England and then getting used to being involved in most of Bunny's business when I had lived full time in Africa.

Whilst Bunny was away, Oney was my companion. Oney and I walked the length of the beach, the sun blazing down on us. Oney was in his twenties, and very talented in his music, with handsome features and a toned body from all his weightlifting. He would chat gaily long into the night about evangelism his big passion. I really enjoyed spending time with Bunny's brothers; they were all so interesting in their own way. I realised I needed to think of them as my own family now that I was becoming African. We watched with amusement as the sailors tried to buy sex with the local girls. There seemed quite an industry there on Tarqwa Bay.

A Rasta boy joined us on the beach and invited us to his home to meet his wife and family living in one of the empty military huts, which were derelict on parts of the island. It was strange still seeing a hut and several buildings that resembled hangers where the soldiers and sailors would have hung out and eaten their food whilst they were convalescing. In fact, one of the buildings still had a sign over it called The Mess.

I knew I had to accept it, but I wasn't looking forward to the strong possibility that in the future Bunny would take at least one other wife, if not more! Would she then want to live in our compound, or would Bunny build her another house? I took the opportunity to talk to Oney about my concerns, but he informed me that as Bunny's first wife, I would have to see his new wife and approve of her. This was all so different from married life in England. The only comforting thought about this was that Bunny and I might have grandchildren. Having gone back to England and reinstated my career, I wondered if I went back to Africa to live and relaunched my sculpting in Agbor and even began teaching the children of the village how to sculpt, would it all be enough for me? I needed something to fill my days and keep busy, as Bunny was only going to get busier; also, it was about finding my position there and keeping busy, you have to know your place when your husband is a chief priest. I realised that Bunny was my life. I felt that we were soulmates, but I just wasn't sure if I could fully become this African woman whom I needed to be.

We had begun a process of paperwork and interviews with immigration to bring Bunny home to England, as he wanted to visit and meet my family. I lay in the sun and tried to rest my mind from all these massive decisions.

The two days passed quicker than expected, as Oney was good company. Two days later, Bunny returned, full of optimism, and never left my side. We made love like there was no tomorrow, making up for the time we'd been apart and the time we'd be away again.

Much too soon it was time for us to head back to the airport. It was planned for me to head back to Blighty and for Bunny to go and organise his father's official funeral.

Once home, I could begin to contemplate the dilemma of my two lives. How could I stay in Oxford alone, without Bunny? Could I give up my British life for him? Could I really trust him? My head ached worrying about it all, and work was often a welcome relief from my confused thoughts.

Many friends and family were asking questions about this strange marriage where we didn't seem to be together, but the whole episode of living and working in Africa, especially living amongst the Igbos, had changed my life. They had become a new family, and it had all made a major impact on my life. They say Africa gets you, and you never forget it. I certainly couldn't. I felt like I'd abandoned them when they needed me. How could I leave them? They seemed so desperate and needy. The education system of having to pay for their children's education when they were extremely poor never left my mind. After witnessing, sickness, famine, corruption, and many more things, learning to adjust to working in the UK again was going to take a long time. But I had stepped back into the familiar world of management in newspapers. It was fast and furious. The paper I was working on was one of the oldest free newspapers in the UK, it was claimed, and had its rules and principles, and my life was so structured compared to the Africans. When I wasn't busy with work, my mind would not stop thinking about Africa and how I might be able to help its people. It was just such a hard job, though. How could one woman save a country from famine, poverty, and corruption?

Even Bunny seemed so out of place there at times, with his modern, Western ways of thinking. His solution was to try and put his views into his songs, to make them freedom songs. It had been said that he was like a new, emerging Bob Marley. All we could do was to keep writing and phoning each other and to try and make progress with his visa to England. I opened this letter from Bunny and felt close again.

Bunny's letter.

*Illah, Delta State,*
*Nigeria*
*December 12ᵗʰ 1997*
  *My dearest wife, kindly accept my deepest apology for not staying with you at the airport till departure time. I know you will understand my situation that very day. I got to Sunday's house around 9:00 p.m., packed up my bags, and then drove to 15, Ojota to catch a bus to Agbor. The bus*

*left Lagos by 11:00 p.m., exactly the same time your plane was taking off. I felt guilty and wept in the bus. I said to myself, what is happening? I am supposed to be saying safe journey to my wife, and here I am alone in the bus, travelling a long distance in the dark. I felt like coming down from the bus and rushing back to the airport to catch a glimpse of you and say goodbye once again, but I remembered that you might be in the air by now flying, 11:15 p.m.*

*Later I realised that my bus was on high speed along the express road and that we were fifty kilometres away from Lagos.*

*I looked around. Everybody behind me in the bus was sleeping. I tried to close my eyes and sleep, but I couldn't. You were all over the place as I closed my eyes. I started weeping again till I started dreaming of both you and I on the beach, trying to buy some oranges. I was still dreaming till a preacher man woke everybody up when he started praying in the name of Jesus. When I looked at my watch, it was 3:25 a.m. We arrived at Benin 4:15 a.m. The driver stopped at a filling station to take some fuel. We all came down from the bus to take twenty minutes' rest. I arrived in Agbor 6:00 a.m., then took my bath and breakfast, and then sent Onochie to get me a taxi. I arrived at Illah 11:00 a.m.*

*On my arrival I met one of the masquerades arriving with more than fifty youths escorting it to Okule, a temporary lodge built by Father's relations to accommodate nine masquerades from all the nine villages that make up Illah. Sylvester told me that two masquerades have earlier arrived. I should change my dress and go to the Okule and greet the elders. He told me that the elders started arriving since 7:00 a.m. and that they have been asking of me because I am supposed to be sitting in the Okule from 6:30 a.m. to receive the elders and all the masquerades. So, I hurriedly say hello to my mother and Mercy's mother. Their heads were shaved the previous night. They were each sitting in their rooms with all the village women sitting around them. I changed my clothes and rushed to the Okule. My seat was vacant. I bowed and greeted the elders. They responded warmly; then I went straight to my chair and sat down. Within five minutes another masquerade arrived from the next village. After the arrival of the fourth masquerade, the senior elder asked me why I was late to the ceremony and that he has acted and played my part before the first masquerade arrived. I stood up and apologised to them, and I told them that I am just coming from Lagos where I had gone to see my wife off at the airport. They immediately agreed and some of them started asking me about you and the reason for your going back to England without watching the king's burial. I told them that you are going back because of your work and that you are the main sponsor of the burial ceremony. They all started to pray for your long life and success in all you do. By 3:00 p.m. the whole village masquerades and all the elders of Illah had arrived. It was a big festival—women cooking, youths dancing around the entire Illah town, gun salute every day for ten days. Dancing and feasting for ten days. Spending and drinking all over.*

*Over the ten days I bought, one hundred gunshots, three hundred cartons of beer, one hundred bottles of hot drinks—for example, schnapps, one hundred gallons of illicit gin, one hundred gallons of palm wine, eight bags of rice, four hundred tubes of yam, six cartons of tin tomatoes, twenty gallons of groundnut oil, ten gallons of red oil, three bags of salt, nine goats and fifteen chickens slaughtered. It was a period of feasting and confusion. I kept calculating money every day until I spent almost all the money you gave to me. The burial took 170,000, naira which we thought will be enough for the burial. The total amount you gave to me was £1,600, which is 208,000 naira. I spent 18,000 naira during your arrival both for transport and all other expenses, so I am left with 20,000 naira, out of which I am sending this letter at the rate of 3,500 naira, balancing 16,500 naira, which is £150. This will keep me till January, but I am very happy that the burial has been performed without any problem, and right now I am very free.*

*All thanks go to you, Sue, for making it possible. May Almighty God bless and protect you, for you are my own forever.*

*Do not let government policies and embassies destroy our love for you are everything to me. Since I met you, my life has changed. This is my first time to know true love. You are woman more than ten men put together.*

*You brought all Illah people together to bury the king. You made me to be very proud at Illah; you brought happiness to me. I cannot stop loving you, my dearest wife. My only regret is that I want to be with you wherever you are, so make sure that I am on my way to England latest Feb.*

*Thanks once more for everything, Sue. I am happy and proud of you, but I don't know how to pay back until I am there with you. I am now at Agbor.*

*Write and tell me about your journey back to England and your work. I hope things are all right with you over there? Extend my greetings to your parents and well-wishers. The moon is out. Look at it in the night and speak to me. I pray every night by watching the moon, by 12:00 a.m., which is 11:00 p.m. over there; come out and receive your prayers.*

*The boy who wanted to sell his land to us stayed ten days with us at Illah. He kept reminding me, but I told him I will only act on my wife's instructions when I hear. Thanks.*

*Lots of Love, Bunny xxxxxx*

# CHAPTER 39

# BUNNY ARRIVES, SEPTEMBER 1999

Today is the day. Bunny flies into England after nearly two years of us keeping in touch via fax and letters and my holiday out to him plus the occasional phone call.

After two years my black prince, a king-to-be, is arriving. It seems that the two years have left their mark on our faces. Oh! Yes, we have changed, but the feelings and the contact never wavered. His trip to England was delayed by many months, initially because of a rejection from the Nigerian Embassy. They refused Bunny's visa because he worked as a musician and chief priest, so they felt he could not support himself in England and was therefore potentially a burden to me and the state.

We had more luck with our second attempt, when I enclosed the last six payslips from my work at the newspaper office, which showed that I'd earned more than enough to look after Bunny until he got a job.

Although that satisfied the bureaucracy, I had my own worries. We needed Bunny to get a job, but what sort of job would a tribal king-to-be do in the UK?

Also, Bunny was not really used to conventional work. His life was one of music, divination, healing, and African traditionalism.

He never even went to the shops for himself; he was used to just sending someone. At least he could cook, as he learned that from his time spent alone in the Gambia. There were so many hurdles to overcome in this relationship, and I had spent long nights praying that our love would be able to conquer all our differences.

My cheap lodgings, where I rented only a room, had enabled me to save for Bunny's arrival, but we needed somewhere different for both of us to live.

Two months before he had arrived, I had found a two-bedroomed house that I had paid the deposit on and moved all my furniture into from Marian's garage. And now we would need to budget, as I had set up home in a quiet village near the Cotswolds, which I knew he would like. I hoped that he would not find it too quiet—although it seemed rather expensive, after renting only a room before in Abingdon. The lodge was a detached house—small and expensive—but it was in a great location at the end of a lane. Plenty of places for Bunny to walk and pray.

It was private and had no streetlights (similar to Africa) and a fantastic view across a farm. The funny thing was the owner of that house was called Mr Landless, yet he seemed to have so much land; it was ironic. The cattle seemed so brown and fat compared to the thin cattle that the Muslim tribesmen cared for in Agbor. I knew Bunny would comment about all those things. I thought of our seasons and their differences from our stay in Africa. I wondered how he would manage in the cold winters, and Bunny had never even seen snow. It was all going to be so exciting and romantic, I thought.

I knew that Bunny was fastidious about being tidy both internally and externally. I made sure everything was clean and tidy before heading off to the airport to meet him.

As I drove to the airport, I thought about all the things he'd notice about good old England with its quirky Englishness.

Red post boxes, joggers, cyclists in bright colours, rain, wind, hail, and the cold weather. Even large estates full of out-of-town shopping malls. Green countryside, wild horses, caravan's gypsies, delicatessen stores. Then there was our culture: music, theatres, art galleries, and museums.

Oxford with its universities, students walking around in black capes and mortar board hats, TV shows, BBC News, politics, NHS, free schools, liberated women. Of course, the pill, liberated gay people, lack of religious activity, English pubs, allotments, Libraries, play groups for children, high-rise flats, English politeness. Queueing in banks, stores and doctors' surgeries. Pets, dog lovers, cat adverts on TV. Then there were policemen walking the street without guns. Bunny was certainly going to see a different world!

The list was endless. I started to get nervous and hoped he would love England. I realised that he would not be a king or chief priest here, just an ordinary Rasta guy. As my father had said in our discussions before his arrival, "He will have no real job prospects and few qualifications, and he will be an immigrant, Sue…err, even a fourth-class citizen here."

"Dad, you haven't met him yet. Give him a chance," I had said.

I knew my father and mother were worried about Bunny and his prospects. They had worked all their lives and had instilled in me the value of employment. But I had to give Bunny all my attention now and encourage and guide him in this idea. I just hoped that Bunny could adjust. Maybe he could even go to college or evening classes, if he cannot find suitable work I thought. I was yet to find out about this part of our lives.

Then I saw him. He was in the queue with many other Africans in their brightly coloured tribal wear, but he stood out.

He was wearing a brown corduroy suit and new shiny shoes, and he'd got beads in his Rasta dreadlocked hair that seemed to almost reach his waist.

So tall, so noble, my prince was finally on English soil. I was so excited.

"Ha-ha, my wife! My wife! Greeting me," said Bunny.

I could not speak because the tears of joy were running down my face. He swung me in the air, and we laughed, oblivious to everyone.

Time to now see if our love could conquer all our differences?

*The Reunion*
*The greeting and meeting*
*Heated exchange of words*
*Remembering where we were*
*Love knows no distance*
*Phone calls and mail saved us*

*We look older*
*Touching nervously*
*In bed together*
*Hot air, pores open, wet bodies*
*Light creeps through curtains*
*Refusing your advances*
*Checking each other's lives*
*Emotions now rising*
*Too late our mouths lock*
*Passions consume us*
*We roll across the bed*
*I am entered, union complete*
*Our bodies glisten with sweat*
*Long into the night we delight*
*Futures now all seem possible*
*My king, my chief, my life,*
*Now my new future, we hope.*

The End

Bunny and I in the Cotswolds.

With Bunny's family in Nigeria

# Interview with the Author

Sue Hadley

Tribal name: Sue Hadley Ugochukwu Anikwe

Bunny Ugochukwu Anikwe

Q: What made you write this book about life and marriage in Nigeria?

A: I really wrote this novel because I wanted to capture an adventure that I was embarking on in West Africa. Also, to inspire other women to have an adventure and take some risks in life and maybe to find their purpose. The book tells you the full story of how I began my diary's first poem right there and then alone on the plane. It was to be the first of many poems and chapters. I wanted to capture the sights and sounds of the places I visited and the people I met during my life in Africa.

Q: You witnessed many strange things living with the Igbo people, even a different religion. Sue, is this religion in Nigeria—African tribal religion— discussed openly in the UK, or do you feel that it's still kept a secret?

*African Tribal Religion* is not really a secret. It's just not so well known. You see, most Nigerians (Africans) who practise this religion mix it with some Christianity and do live a kind of Biblical way of life, although they still slaughter animals like goats at the shrine and have fetishes, plus do dancing. They often then go into trance and also believe in and use divination. But this is all part of the African way of life.

Q: Do you now understand its beginnings?

Yes, you see Ancient Yoruba and Igbo people believed that the world was formed by the gods and people came from water and earth to exist together and survive on earth. But of course, you and I know that cultures do evolve and things change.

Q: What do you think people will learn from your adventure?

I think they will learn that life is there for the taking. I believe it's important to embrace all cultures and remain open to new people and to always keep learning.

Q: Did you realise what life was going to be like there in Nigeria and what my religion and culture would involve?

When I met you in the Gambia, you were a struggling "Rasta musician," who was trying as a singer with his band to make his style of reggae and high-life music work in the Gambia. No, I did not realise what Nigeria and your religion and culture would be like

Q: What is your plan now, Sue?

Put this book for sale worldwide and continue to write. I need to write my next book about the Tribal Awucha religion and all its customs. It will be called Tribal *Cures* and include your life Bunny in UK, plus the funny stories and cures chiefs use both abroad and, in the UK, past and presently.

I feel it would be good to make a film about this true Nigerian-English romantic story too.

Q: Do you have many mixed marriages there in UK now?

Many people are now experiencing mixed marriages worldwide, and often the women are older than their men I've noticed. Watch out for my next book.

The Shrine in Agbor

# THE AUTHOR

Sue Hadley grew up in the West Midlands as a typical Black Country girl. But she had a thirst for adventure and travel. She studied many subjects and gained many qualifications. But It seems that throughout her life, her experiences and prophetic dreams and insights made her soon admit that she had inherited the 'gift,' a trait she fought avidly, but it led her to seek adventure in Africa in order to find people who shared the idea of divination, self-discovery. The book takes us on an adventure across Africa where in her search, she finds her prince but all is not what it seems. But now having lived as the only white woman amongst the Igbo people she has learnt many things. Sue is a certified Life & Business Coaches Coach and has taught over 300 adults to change their lives for the better. She continues to teach both Counselling and Life Coaching plus Neuro Linguistic Programming at Oxford Colleges

Watch out for her second Book *Tribal Cures* and grasp her insights.

Contact the author: suehadleyhadders@gmail.com

Printed by Amazon Italia Logistica S.r.l.
Torrazza Piemonte (TO), Italy

47847776R00125